COPYCAT RECIPES

The complete cookbook with Simple and Delicious Ideas for Beginners

William Oliver Thomas

Copyright - 2020 - by William Oliver Thomas
All rights reserved.

The content contained within this book may not be reproduced, duplicated or transmitted without direct written permission from the author or the publisher. Under no circumstances will any blame or legal responsibility be held against the publisher, or author, for any damages, reparation, or monetary loss due to the information contained within this book. Either directly or indirectly.

Legal Notice:

This book is copyright protected. This book is only for personal use. You cannot amend, distribute, sell, use, quote or paraphrase any part, or the content within this book, without the consent of the author or publisher.

Disclaimer Notice:

Please note the information contained within this document is for educational and entertainment purposes only. All effort has been executed to present accurate, up to date, and reliable, complete information. No warranties of any kind are declared or implied. Readers acknowledge that the author is not engaging in the rendering of legal, financial, medical or professional advice. The content within this book has been derived from various sources. Please consult a licensed professional before attempting any techniques outlined in this book.

By reading this document, the reader agrees that under no circumstances is the author responsible for any losses, direct or indirect, which are incurred as a result of the use of information contained within this document, including, but not limited to, - errors, omissions, or inaccuracies.

TABLE OF CONTENTS

INTRODUCTION	7
CHAPTER 1	
SIDE SALAD RECIPES	9
1. EGGPLANT PARMESAN	10
2. LASAGNA FRITTA	11
3. FRIED MOZZARELLA	12
4. GNOCCHI WITH SPICY TOMATO AND WINE SAUCE	13
5. BRUSSELS SPROUT N' KALE SALAD	14
6. BREADED FRIED OKRA	15
7. OLIVE GARDEN SALAD	16
8. ESPERANZA HOUSE SALAD	17
9. SPINACH APPLE SALAD	18
10. ANYTHING AND EVERYTHING SALAD	19
11. CHILI'S SALAD	20
12. CRACKER BARREL FRIED APPLES	21
13. HASH BROWN CASSEROLE	22
14. CUCUMBERS, TOMATOES, AND ONIONS	23
15. OLD COUNTRY STORE BABY CARROTS	24
16. HOUSE SALAD AND DRESSING	25
17. SANTA FE CRISPERS SALAD	26
18. QUESADILLA EXPLOSION SALAD	27
19. CARIBBEAN SHRIMP SALAD	28
20. SOUTHWEST CAESAR SALAD	29
21. RED BEANS FROM POPEYE'S	30
22. CAFÉ RIO'S SWEET PORK BARBACOA SALAD	31
23. ALMOND CRUSTED SALMON SALAD	32
24. DEEP FRIED PICKLES FROM TEXAS ROADHOUSE	33
25. CHILI'S CHILI	34
26. HAM SALAD	35
27. ITALIAN B.M.T. ® SALAD	36
28. ROASTED CHICKEN SALAD	37
29. ROAST BEEF SALAD	38
30. STEAK & CHEESE SALAD	39
31. SUBWAY CLUB ® SALAD	40
32. SUBWAY MELT ® SALAD	41
33. CHICKEN TERIYAKI SALAD	42
34. TUNA SALAD	43
35. TURKEY SALAD	44
CHAPTER 2	
OLD AND MODERN SWEET AND SAVORY SNACK RECIPES	45
36. ROADHOUSE MASHED POTATOES	46
37. SWEET POTATOES WITH MARSHMALLOWS AND CARAMEL SAUCE	47
38. SAUTÉED MUSHROOMS	48
39. HAM AND CHEESE EMPANADAS	49
40. ROADHOUSE GREEN BEANS	50
41. ROADHOUSE CHEESE FRIES	51
42. DINNER ROLLS	52
43. TEXAS RED CHILI	53
44. BONELESS BUFFALO WINGS	54
45. TATER SKINS	55
46. FRIED PICKLES	56
47. RATTLESNAKE BITES	57
48. CACTUS BLOSSOM	58
49. CRISPY CHEESY CHIPS	59
50. BRINED CHICKEN BITES	60

51. BLOOMIN' ONION	61
52. PEPPERONI CHIPS	62
53. MAC 'N CHEESE	63
54. RED LOBSTER FUDGE OVERBOARD	64
55. CHOCOLATE WAVE	65
56. HOUSTON'S APPLE WALNUT COBBLER	66
57. PAPA JOHN'S CINNAPIE	67
58. OLIVE GARDEN'S CHEESE ZITI AL FORNO	68
59. CHIPOTLE'S REFRIED BEANS	69
60. LOW FAT VEGGIE QUESADILLA	70
61. GARLIC MASHED POTATOES	71
62. VEGETABLE MEDLEY	72
63. MEGA MANGO SMOOTHIE	73
64. LASAGNA WITH FETA AND BLACK OLIVES	74
65. EASY COPYCAT MONTEREY'S LITTLE MEXICO QUESO	75
66. FRIED KETO CHEESE WITH MUSHROOMS	76
67. MUSHROOM RECIPE STUFFED WITH CHEESE, SPINACH, AND BACON	77
68. SHRIMP NACHOS WITH AVOCADO AND TOMATO SALSA	78
69. MIMOSA EGGS WITH TRUFFLE	79
70. SHRIMP TEMPURA	80
71. COPYCAT CHILI'S SOUTHWEST EGG ROLLS	81
72. HAM AND CHEESE GRINDERS	82
73. MOZZARELLA CHEESE STICKS RECIPE	83
74. COPYCAT MAC AND CHEESE WITH SMOKED GOUDA CHEESE AND PUMPKIN	84
75. BAKED BUFFALO MEATBALLS	85

CHAPTER 3	
OLD AND MODERN FRUIT SALAD RECIPES	**87**
76. APPLE POMEGRANATE SALAD: WENDY'S™ COPYCAT	88
77. CRANBERRY FRUIT SALAD: THE FAMOUS LUBY'S CAFETERIA™ COPYCAT	89
78. FUJI APPLE CHICKEN SALAD: PANERA BREAD™ COPYCAT	90
79. MARKET SALAD: CHICK-FIL-A™ COPYCAT	91
80. STRAWBERRY POPPYSEED SALAD: PANERA™ COPYCAT	92
81. SWEET CARROT SALAD: CHICK-FIL-A™ COPYCAT	93
82. WALDORF SALAD: TEXAS LUBY'S CAFETERIA™ COPYCAT	94
83. COTTAGE CHEESE AND POPPY SEED MOUSSE WITH CHERRY WATER	95
84. GOOD MOOD FRUIT SALAD	96
85. FRUIT SALAD WITH LEMON FOAM	97
86. VEGAN AMARANTH PUDDING WITH FRUIT SALAD	98
87. QUICK FRUIT SALAD WITH SABAYON	99
88. TROPICAL FRUIT SALAD WITH COCONUT CREAM	100
89. EXOTIC FRUIT SALAD WITH COCONUT-LIME YOGHURT	101
90. GINGER FRUIT SALAD WITH VANILLA SAUCE	102
91. FRUIT SALAD WITH VANILLA SAUCE	103
92. FRUIT SALAD WITH YOGHURT CREAM	104

CHAPTER 4
OLD AND MODERN
DESSERT RECIPES **105**

93. MAPLE BUTTER BLONDIE 106
94. MAPPLE CHIMI CHEESECAKE 107
95. TRIPLE CHOCOLATE MELTDOWN 108
96. CHOCOLATE MOUSSE DESSERT SHOOTER 109
97. DEADLY CHOCOLATE SIN 110
98. ORANGE CREAMSICLE CAKE 111
99. CINNAMON APPLE TURNOVER 112
100. BURGER KING'S HERSHEY'S SUNDAE PIE 113
101. CHILI'S CHOCOLATE BROWNIE SUNDAE 114
102. BEN & JERRY'S CHERRY GARCIA ICE CREAM 115
103. P.F. CHANG'S COCONUT PINEAPPLE ICE CREAM WITH BANANA SPRING ROLLS 116
104. TGI FRIDAY'S OREO MADNESS 117
105. BEN & JERRY'S CHUNKY MONKEY ICE CREAM 118
106. JACK IN THE BOX'S OREO COOKIE SHAKE 119
107. DAIRY QUEEN'S CANDY CANE CHILL 120
108. DAIRY QUEEN'S BLIZZARD 121
109. APPLEBEE'S MAPLE BUTTER BLONDIE 122
110. HOUSTON'S APPLE WALNUT COBBLER 123
111. MELTING POT CHOCOLATE FONDUE 124
112. P.F. CHANG'S GINGER PANNA COTTA 125
113. STARBUCKS' CRANBERRY BLISS BARS 126
114. OLIVE GARDEN'S TIRAMISU 127
115. MAPLE BUTTER BLONDIE 128
116. CHEF JOHN'S ZABAGLIONE 129
117. CHOCOLATE MOUSSE DESSERT SHOOTER 130
118. CINNAMON APPLE TURNOVER 131
119. CHERRY CHOCOLATE COBBLER 132
120. PUMPKIN CUSTARD WITH GINGERSNAPS 133
121. BAKED APPLE DUMPLINGS 134
122. PEACH COBBLER 135
123. CAMPFIRE S'MORES 136
124. BANANA PUDDING 137
125. CHILI'S NEW YORK STYLE CHEESECAKE 138
126. STARBUCK'S COPYCAT CRANBERRY CHOCOLATE BLISS BARS 139
127. CHOCOLATE PECAN 140
128. PEANUT BUTTER KISSES 141
129. PEANUT BUTTER & PECAN NUT CHEESECAKE 142
130. THREE-INGREDIENT CHOCOLATE MACADAMIA FAT BOMBS 144
131. GOAT CHEESE WITH STEWED BLACKBERRIES 145
132. RHUBARB TART 146
133. SAFFRON PANNA COTTA 147

CHAPTER 5
OLD AND MODERN
PASTRY RECIPES **149**

134. CHESS PIE 150
135. COCONUT CREAM PIE BARS 151
136. CREAMY HAZELNUT PIE 152
137. THE FAMOUS WOOLWORTH ICE BOX CHEESECAKE 153

#	Recipe	Page
138.	FROZEN BANANA SPLIT PIE	154
139.	FROZEN PEACH PIE	155
140.	KEY LIME PIE	156
141.	STRAWBERRY LEMONADE FREEZER PIE	157
142.	SWEET POTATO PIE	158
143.	BLUEBERRY SOUR CREAM POUND CAKE	159
144.	CARROT CAKE DELIGHT	160
145.	FOUR LAYER PUMPKIN CAKE WITH FROSTING	161
146.	GEORGIA PEACH POUND CAKE	162
147.	PINEAPPLE PECAN CAKE WITH FROSTING	163
148.	RED VELVET CAKE	164
149.	PUMPKIN CHEESECAKE	165
150.	REESE'S PEANUT BUTTER CHOCOLATE CAKE CHEESECAKE	166
151.	WHITE CHOCOLATE RASPBERRY SWIRL CHEESECAKE	168
152.	CARROT CAKE CHEESECAKE	169
153.	ORIGINAL CHEESECAKE	170
154.	ULTIMATE RED VELVET CHEESECAKE	171
155.	STRAWBERRY SHORTCAKE	173
156.	LEMONCELLO CREAM TORTE	174
157.	OREO COOKIE CHEESECAKE	175
158.	BANANA CREAM CHEESECAKE	176
159.	BLACKOUT CAKE	177
160.	MOLTEN LAVA CAKE	178
161.	WHITE CHOCOLATE RASPBERRY NOTHING BUNDT CAKES	180
162.	CARAMEL ROCKSLIDE BROWNIES	181
163.	CORNBREAD MUFFINS	182
164.	CHOCOLATE MOUSSE CAKE	183
165.	BLACKBERRY AND APPLES COBBLER	184
166.	BLACK TEA CAKE	185
167.	QUINOA MUFFINS	186
168.	FIGS PIE	187

CHAPTER 6
SOFT DRINK RECIPES **189**

#	Recipe	Page
169.	LEMON AND BERRY SLUSH	190
170.	TACO BELL'S PENA COLADA DRINK	191
171.	CHICK FIL-A LEMONADE	192
172.	DAIRY QUEEN BLIZZARD	193
173.	WATERMELON AND MINT LEMONADE	194
174.	SONIC OCEAN WATER	195
175.	RAINFOREST CAFÉ'S STRAWBERRY LEMONADE	196
176.	CHICK-FIL-A'S FROZEN LEMONADE COPYCAT	197
177.	DUNKIN DONUT'S MINT HOT CHOCOLATE COPYCAT	198
178.	TIM HORTON'S HOT APPLE CIDER COPYCAT	199
179.	NEW ORLEANS' FAMOUS HURRICANES COPYCAT	200
180.	RUBY TUESDAY'S RASPBERRY ICED TEA COPYCAT	201
181.	MIKE'S HARD LEMONADE COPYCAT	202
182.	CHICK-FIL-A'S FROSTED LEMONADE COPYCAT	203
183.	CRYSTAL LIGHT'S BERRY SANGRIA MIX COPYCAT	204

CHAPTER 7
PRACTICAL ADVICE FOR BEGINNERS TO CANNING AND PRESERVING YOUR FAVORITE FOODS **205**

CONCLUSION **209**

Introduction

Are you always looking forward to making delicious foods from breakfast to dinner? Copycat recipes practically give you the ability to make great restaurant food tasting in your own home and get it the right first time and easily. Make delicious copies of the food that you always love from the restaurant's menu when dining with your family and friends.

The copycat recipes are so popular today that they are being written by several people all around the world with great content and of a high standard. Most people around the world love to eat delicious foods in a restaurant, and they hope that they will find the same recipes being served at home.

Nowadays, most people are making copycat recipes in their home when they are preparing food for their family and friends. When you are using the copycat recipe, there are a few steps that should be modified with the recipes that have already been written before.

It is important to follow the steps that have already been written before with the copycat recipe. It is essential to read the steps which have already been written before and mix the ingredients in the right proportion. Some people always feel that they will follow extra steps and modify the copycat recipe, but you should be careful when you are modifying the copycat recipe to make amazing delicious dishes at home. An individual must follow the steps correctly, and following the correct steps will make it easy for the individuals to get the recipe and make the delicious dishes in their homes. The following tips will help you to make the copycat recipes in your home with the utmost taste and enjoyment.

Get all the ingredients required for the recipe and make sure you have followed the proper quantity. You should ensure that you have the right items for your recipe and they are present in the required amount. If you are baking a cake and you are using batter, you should make sure that you have all the ingredients that you are required, and they are present in the required amount. This book has the most excellent copycat recipes from different restaurants around the world.

Chapter 1

Side Salad Recipes

1. Eggplant Parmesan

Preparation Time: 2 h 15'

Servings: 2-4

Cooking Time: 10'

Ingredients

- 1 medium Italian eggplant, peeled and cut into ½-inch slices
- 2 teaspoons kosher salt
- ½ cup all-purpose flour
- 1 cup eggs, beaten
- 2 cups Italian breadcrumbs
- ½ cup vegetable oil
- ¾ cup marinara sauce
- ¼ cup basil-infused olive oil
- 3 tablespoons Parmesan cheese, grated, divided
- 4 ounces mozzarella cheese, grated
- 1/8 teaspoon kosher salt
- 5 ounces angel hair pasta, cooked
- ½ teaspoon parsley, chopped

Directions

1. Preheat the oven to broil. Line a baking sheet with paper towels. Season both sides of the eggplant circles with salt and arrange them on the pan. Cover the eggplant with another sheet of paper towel and refrigerate for 2 hours.
2. Place the flour in one bowl, the eggs in another, and the breadcrumbs in a third bowl.
3. After 2 hours, remove the eggplant from the fridge and dry the slices with a fresh paper towel. One at a time, dip the slices in flour, then in the egg, and finally in the breadcrumbs. Set them aside.
4. Cook the oil in a large skillet over medium heat. Fry the eggplant for about 2 minutes on each side and set them on a plate lined with a paper towel.
5. Cook the marinara sauce in a small saucepan and the basil oil in another small pan.
6. Place a wire rack in a baking dish and transfer the cooked eggplant slices to the rack. Sprinkle on 2 tablespoons of the Parmesan cheese and the mozzarella, then put the pan under the broiler until the cheese melts.
7. Serve the cooked pasta topped with eggplant. Pour some marinara over the top. Drizzle basil oil and sprinkle with the remaining Parmesan cheese and parsley.

Nutrition: 230 Calories 14g Total Fat 17.1g Carbs 8g Protein

2. Lasagna Fritta

Preparation Time: 20'

Servings: 14

Cooking Time: 4'

Ingredients

- 2/3 + ¼ cup milk (divided)
- 1 cup grated parmesan cheese, plus some more for serving
- ¾ cup feta cheese
- ¼ teaspoon white pepper
- 1 tablespoon butter
- 7 lasagna noodles
- 1 egg
- Breadcrumbs
- Oil for frying
- 2 tablespoons marinara sauce
- Alfredo sauce, for serving

Directions

1. Place the butter, white pepper, ☐ cup milk, parmesan, and feta cheese in a pot. Stir and boil. Make lasagna noodles as stated on the package.
2. Spread a thin layer of the cheese and milk mixture on each noodle. Fold into 2-inch pieces and place something heavy on top to keep them folded. Place in the freezer for at least 1 hour, then cut each noodle in half lengthwise.
3. In a small bowl, mix the ¼ cup milk and egg together. In another bowl, place breadcrumbs. Dip each piece into the egg wash, then the breadcrumbs. Fry the noodles at 350°F for 4 minutes.
4. Serve by spreading some alfredo sauce at the bottom of the plate, placing the lasagna on top, and then drizzling with marinara sauce. Sprinkle the grated parmesan cheese

Nutrition: 1070 Calories 71g Total Fat 73g Carbs 35g Protein

3. Fried Mozzarella

Preparation Time: 10'

Servings: 4

Cooking Time: 10'

Ingredients

- 1-pound mozzarella or other cheese
- 2 eggs, beaten
- ¼ cup water
- 1½ cups Italian breadcrumbs
- ½ teaspoons garlic salt
- 1 teaspoon Italian seasoning
- 2/3 cup flour
- 1/3 cup cornstarch

Directions

1. Slice thick cuts of the cheese. Blend together eggs and water for egg wash. Combine the breadcrumbs, garlic salt, and Italian seasoning. In another bowl, combine together flour and cornstarch.
2. Cook vegetable oil in a frying pan. Soak each piece of cheese into the flour, then egg wash, then breadcrumbs. Deep fry until golden brown. Set aside and drain on a paper towel. Serve with marinara sauce.

Nutrition: 100.8 Calories 5.7g Total Fat 7g Carbs 4g Protein

4. Gnocchi with Spicy Tomato and Wine Sauce

Preparation Time: 10'

Servings: 4

Cooking Time: 40'

Ingredients

Sauce
- 2 tablespoons extra virgin olive oil
- 6 fresh garlic cloves
- ½ teaspoon chili flakes
- 1 cup dry white wine
- 1 cup chicken broth
- 2 cans (14.5 ounces each) tomatoes
- ¼ cup fresh basil, chopped
- ¼ cup sweet creamy butter, cut into 1-inch cubes, chilled
- ½ cup parmesan cheese, freshly grated

Pasta
- 1-pound gnocchi
- Salt, to taste
- Black pepper, freshly crushed, to taste

Directions

1. Sauté the olive oil, garlic, and chili flakes in a cold pan over medium heat. When the garlic starts turning golden brown, stir in the wine and broth and let it simmer.
2. When the broth simmers down. Mix in the tomatoes and basil and then continue simmering for another 30 minutes. Once thickened, let it rest for 3 minutes.
3. After a few minutes, transfer the sauce in a blender, and stir in the butter and parmesan. Purée and set aside. Make the pasta by boiling the gnocchi in a large pot. When it is cooked, drain the pasta and blend the sauce. Serve.

Nutrition: 320.7 Calories 22.5g Total Fat 11.6g Carbs 12.8g Protein

5. Brussels Sprout N' Kale Salad

| Preparation Time: | 5' | | Servings: | 4-6 |

| Cooking Time: | 1 |

Ingredients

- 1 bunch kale
- 1-pound Brussels sprouts
- ¼ cup craisins (or dry cranberries)
- ½ cup pecans, chopped
- Maple vinaigrette
- ½ cup olive oil
- ¼ cup apple cider vinegar
- ¼ cup maple syrup
- 1 teaspoon dry mustard

Directions

1. Cut the kale and brussels sprouts with a mandolin slicer. Transfer to a salad bowl. Add the pecans to a skillet on high heat. Toast for 60 seconds, then transfer to the salad bowl.
2. Add the craisins. Mix all the ingredients for the vinaigrette and whisk to combine. Dash the vinaigrette over the salad and toss. Refrigerate for a few hours or preferably overnight before serving.

Nutrition: 37.8 Calories 0.26g Total Fat 7.88g Carbs 2.97g Protein 1g Fiber

6. Breaded Fried Okra

Preparation Time: 15'

Servings: 4

Cooking Time: 10'

Ingredients

- 1-pound fresh okra, rinsed and dried
- 1 cup self-rising cornmeal
- ½ cup self-rising flour
- 1 teaspoon salt
- 1 cup vegetable oil (for frying)
- Salt and pepper to taste

Directions

1. Cook the oil in a large skillet or deep fryer. Cut the okra into ½-inch pieces. Combine the cornmeal, flour, and salt in a large bowl. Drop the okra pieces into the bowl and toss to coat. Allow to rest for a few minutes while the oil heats up.
2. Using a slotted spoon, transfer the okra from the bowl into the hot oil. Cook for about 10 minutes or until the okra has turned a nice golden color.
3. Remove from oil and place on a plate lined with paper towels to drain. Season to taste with salt and pepper.

Nutrition: 18 Calories 3.6g Carbs 1g Protein 2g Fiber

7. Olive Garden Salad

Preparation Time: 15'

Servings: 4

Cooking Time: 0'

Ingredients

- ¼ cup extra-virgin olive oil
- 2 tablespoons white wine vinegar
- 3 tablespoons Miracle Whip
- 1 tablespoon fresh lemon juice
- 2 tablespoons grated parmesan cheese
- ¼ teaspoon garlic salt
- ½ teaspoon dried Italian seasoning
- 1 (10-oz.) bag American salad blend
- ¼ red onion, thinly sliced
- 4 small pepperoncini or other pickled peppers
- 1 small vine-ripened tomato, cut into wedges
- 2 tablespoons sliced black olives
- 1 tablespoon grated parmesan cheese

Directions

1. At first, prepare the salad dressing in a blender. Add olive oil, lemon juice, Miracle Whip, garlic salt, parmesan, water, and Italian seasoning.
2. Hit the pulse button and blend the dressing until all the ingredients are well combined. Pour the dressing into a sealable jar and cover the lid.
3. Place this dressing in the refrigerator for about 1 hour. Meanwhile, prepare the salad in a salad bowl.
4. Prepare the veggies, chop the red onion, cut the tomatoes, slice the cheese, and pepperoncini, one by one on the cutting board. Add red onion, tomato, cheese, olives, and pepperoncini to the salad bowl.
5. Toss them gently with a spatula, then slowly pour in the prepared dressing while leaving half of the dressing for serving.
6. Give the salad a stir, and mix well to coat the veggies. Transfer the salad to the serving plates. Pour the reserved dressing over the salad. Garnish as desired and serve.

Nutrition: 153 Calories 8.9g Total Fat 17g Carbs 2.9g Protein 3.5g Fiber

8. Esperanza House Salad

Preparation Time: 20'

Servings: 4

Cooking Time: 0'

Ingredients

- 8 cups torn lettuce/ greens - 2 cups red cabbage, shredded
- ½ cup carrots, shredded - ½ cup red onions, shredded
- ½ cup green peppers, shredded
- ½ cup mushrooms, sliced
- ½ cup mozzarella cheese, shredded
- ½ cup black olives, shredded
- ½ cup tomatoes, cubed
- ½ cup ham, cubed
- ½ cup sprouts

Esperanza Dressing
- 1 egg yolk - 1/3 cup white vinegar
- 2 tablespoons water
- 1 tablespoon Dijon mustard
- 1 teaspoon Worcestershire sauce
- 1 tablespoon dried onion flakes
- 1 teaspoon granulated garlic
- 1 teaspoon oregano
- ¾ teaspoon salt
- ¼ teaspoon black pepper
- 1 ½ cups soybean oil
- 2 tablespoons minced fresh parsley

Directions

1. Prepare the Esperanza dressing for the salad in a small bowl.
2. Beat the egg yolk in a bowl with an electric mixer until the egg yolk turns pale in color.
3. Add vinegar, salt, black pepper, parsley, soybean oil, oregano, water, garlic, onion flakes, Dijon mustard, and Worcestershire sauce.
4. Whisk this mixture well and cover this salad dressing Transfer the salad dressing to the refrigerator Leave this dressing in the refrigerator until the salad is ready to serve.
5. Now prepare the salad ingredients and place the lettuce leaves on the cutting board.
6. Cut the lettuce leaves into thin slices and keep them aside in the salad bowl Now shred the cabbage on the cutting board and transfer to the salad bowl. Similarly, shred and chop all other vegetables, ham, and mushroom, then add them to the bowl.
7. Add ½ of the prepared dressing to the salad and preserve the other half in the refrigerator. Toss the vegetables well and garnish with olives. Serve fresh.

Nutrition: 250 Calories 16g Total Fat 11g Carbs 12.1g Protein

9. Spinach Apple Salad

Preparation Time: 10'

Servings: 4

Cooking Time: 0

Ingredients

- 6 cups fresh spinach leaves
- ½ cup dried cranberries
- ½ cup feta cheese, crumbled
- ½ cup red apple, chopped
- 1/3 cup honey almonds
- Honey Poppy Seed Dressing
- 2/3 cup vegetable oil
- ½ cup honey
- 4 tablespoons apple cider vinegar
- 1 ½ tablespoons poppy seeds

Directions

1. Prepare the honey poppy seed dressing for the salad in a small bowl Beat honey with vegetable oil in a bowl with a hand mixer Add apple cider vinegar to the honey mixture then add poppy seeds to the honey mixture
2. Whisk this mixture well and cover this salad dressing Transfer the salad dressing to the refrigerator Leave this dressing in the refrigerator until the salad is ready to serve
3. Now prepare the salad ingredients and place the spinach leaves on the cutting board
4. Cut the fresh spinach leaves into small pieces and keep them aside in the salad bowl
5. Now place the apples on the cutting board and core the apples
6. Cut the apples into small cubes then transfer to the salad bowl. Add ¼ of the prepared dressing to the salad Toss in olives and mix well. Serve fresh.

Nutrition: 161.1 Calories 13.3g Total Fat 9.6g Carbs 4.1g Protein

10. Anything and Everything Salad

Preparation Time: 20'

Servings: 4

Cooking Time: 2H 10'

Ingredients

- 6 eggs, beaten
- 1/3 cup sugar
- 1/3 cup apple cider vinegar
- 1 teaspoon salt, or to taste
- 4 cups of elbow macaroni, cooked
- 3 large hard-boiled eggs, peeled and diced
- 1 ¼ cup of ham, cooked
- 1 cup (4 oz.) of diced cheese, melted
- 2 celery chops, sliced thinly
- 1 medium onion, chopped
- ¾ cup sweet pickle sauce
- ¾ cup of olives stuffed with pepper
- 1/3 cup mayonnaise

Directions

1. In a saucepan, mix eggs, beaten, sugar, vinegar, and salt cook and stir over low heat for approximately 10 minutes until the egg mixture thickens and a thermometer indicates 160° F.
2. Allow cooling completely, stirring several times. In a bowl, mix the pasta, boiled eggs, ham, cheese, celery, onion, pickle sauce, and olives. Mix the mayonnaise in the cooled egg mixture.
3. Pour over the pasta mixture. Stir to coat-cover and cool in a refrigerator for at least 2 hours.

Nutrition: 680 Calories 39g Total Fat 17g Carbs 68g Protein 3g Fiber

11. Chili's Salad

Preparation Time: 25'

Servings: 4

Cooking Time: 15'

Ingredients

For Pico De Gallo:
- 2 teaspoon seeded jalapeno peppers, finely diced
- ½ cup red onion finely minced
- 2 medium tomatoes diced very small
- 2 teaspoon cilantro, fresh & finely minced

For Salad:
- 4 chicken breasts skinless, boneless
- 5 ounces bag half-and-half spring mix with baby spinach
- ½ cup red cabbage chopped
- ounces bag butter bliss lettuce or romaine or iceberg lettuce
- ¾ cup raisins
- 1 cup fresh pineapple chunked
- ¼ cup teriyaki sauce
- 14 ounces can mandarin orange segments drained
- Tortilla strips
- ¼ cup water
- For Honey-Lime Dressing:
- 1 cup vanilla Greek yogurt
- ¼ cup Dijon mustard
- 1 tablespoon lime juice, freshly squeezed
- 3 tablespoon apple cider vinegar
- 1 cup honey
- 2 tablespoon sesame oil
- ½ to 1 teaspoon lime zest grated

Directions

For Pico De Gallo:
1. Combine the ingredients for Pico de Gallo together in a small bowl & let chill in a refrigerator until ready to use.

For Salad:
2. Mix the teriyaki sauce with water. Place the chicken pieces in a large-sized plastic bag or plastic bowl. Add in the prepared teriyaki mixture & let marinate for an hour or two in the refrigerator.
3. Layer the lettuce & spring mix in a large serving bowl. Add raisins and cabbage toss well.
4. Refrigerate until all ingredients are ready. After chicken has marinated, lightly coat your grill with the cooking spray and heat it over moderate heat. Remove the chicken pieces from marinade, shaking off any excess.
5. Add to the hot grill & cook until the chicken is cooked through, for 5 to 10 minutes on each side. Slice chicken down into cubes or thin strips. Set aside on the serving plate to serve.
6. For Honey-Lime Dressing:
7. Combine the entire salad dressing ingredients in a blender blend on high until blended well. Refrigerate until ready to serve.

To Assemble the Salad:
8. Remove the salad to four individual large serving plates. Place approximately ¼ cup of the mandarin orange segments & pineapple over each salad.
9. Spread a spoonful or two of Pico de Gallo onto the chicken. Drizzle with salad dressing, give the ingredients a good stir until mixed well.
10. Garnish with the tortilla strips. Serve immediately & enjoy.

Nutrition: 640 Calories 41g Total Fat 44g Carbs 24g Protein 6g Fiber

12. Cracker Barrel Fried Apples

Preparation Time: 10'

Servings: 8

Cooking Time: 20'

Ingredients

- Melt the butter or bacon drippings in a large skillet. Evenly spread the apples at the bottom of the skillet. Sprinkle the lemon juice on top, followed by salt and brown sugar.
- Cover with the lid and cook over low heat for about fifteen minutes, or until the apples are juicy and tender. Sprinkle the nutmeg and cinnamon on top and serve. You may add a squeeze of lemon on top if desired.

Directions

1. Take a medium saucepan, place it over low heat, add butter and erythritol and then cook for 4 to 5 minutes until butter melts and turns golden brown.
2. Stir in cream, bring it to a gentle boil and then simmer the sauce for 10 minutes until the sauce has thickened to coat the back of the spoon, stirring constantly.
3. Remove pan from heat, stir in vanilla extract and then serve.

Nutrition: 78 Calories 15mg Cholestero 17g Carbs

13. Hash Brown Casserole

Preparation Time: 10'

Servings: 10

Cooking Time: 45'

Ingredients

- Nonstick cooking spray
- 2 pounds Hash browns
- 2 cups Shredded Colby cheese or cheddar cheese
- 8 oz Sour cream
- Salt and pepper
- ½ cup Minced onion
- 4 oz Butter
- 10.75 oz Condensed cream of chicken soup

Directions

1. Heat the oven to 350 degrees F. Oil a 9-by-13-inch baking pan. Spread the potatoes into the pan – season with pepper and salt. Add the butter into a microwave-safe dish and microwave until the butter gets melted.
2. Add the sour cream, onions, and sour cream into the bowl and mix thoroughly. Pour the mixture over the potatoes in the pan and sprinkle the cheese on top. Place the pan in the oven to bake for approx. 45 minutes, or until the potatoes are completely warm and the cheese starts to melt.

Nutrition: 321 Calories 8g Protein 19g Carbs 23g Fat

14. Cucumbers, Tomatoes, and Onions

Preparation Time: 10'

Servings: 6

Cooking Time: 10'

Ingredients

- 2 tbsp Italian dressing
- 3 Cucumbers
- 16 oz Grape tomatoes
- ½ cup Sliced white onion
- ½ cup Sugar
- 1 cup White vinegar

Directions

1. Slice the three cucumbers into ¼-inch thin slices. Mix the Italian dressing, sugar, and vinegar in a bowl, then add the sliced onions, tomatoes, and sliced cucumbers.
2. Cover with a foil or a lid and set aside for approx. one hour for the vegetable to marinate before you serve.

Nutrition: 120 Calories 1g Protein 24g Carbs 1g Fat

15. Old Country Store Baby Carrots

| Preparation Time: | 10' | Servings: | 8 |

| Cooking Time: | 45' |

Ingredients

- 2 lbs. Fresh baby carrots
- 1 tbsp Brown sugar
- 2 tbsp Margarine
- 1 pinch Ground nutmeg
- 1 tsp Salt

Directions

1. Rinse the carrots and place them in a 2-quart saucepan. Add water to the pot, enough to cover the carrots. Place the lid on the pan and bring to a boil over medium heat.
2. Reduce the heat to low and simmer for about 30 to 45 minutes, or until the carrots are tender when pricked with a fork.
3. Discard half of the water in the saucepan, then add salt, sugar, and margarine into the pan. Replace the lid on the pan and cook until soft but not mushy. Add more salt if needed. Add the ground nutmeg for a little flair, if desired.

Nutrition: 71 Calories 10g Carbs 3g Fat

16. House Salad and Dressing

Preparation Time: 10'

Servings: 12

Cooking Time: 0'

Ingredients

Salad
- 1 head iceberg lettuce
- ¼ small red onion, sliced thin
- 6–12 black olives, pitted
- 6 pepperoncini
- 2 small roma tomatoes, sliced
- Croutons
- ¼ cup shredded or grated Romano or parmesan cheese Dressing
- 1 packet Italian dressing mix
- ¾ cup vegetable/canola oil
- ¼ cup olive oil
- 1 tablespoon mayonnaise
- 1/3 cup white vinegar
- ¼ cup water
- ½ teaspoon sugar
- ½ teaspoon dried Italian seasoning
- ½ teaspoon salt
- ¼ teaspoon pepper
- ¼ teaspoon garlic powder

Directions

1. To make the dressing, combine all ingredients in a small bowl. Thoroughly whisk together. Refrigerate for 1 hour to marinate. Add the salad ingredient to a salad bowl. When ready to serve, add some of the dressing to the salad and toss to coat. Add grated cheese as a garnish as desired. Store remaining dressing in an airtight container. Keep refrigerated, and it can be stored for up to 3 weeks.

Nutrition: 435 Calories 54.8g Fat 46.4g Carbs 13.9g Protein

17. Santa Fe Crispers Salad

| Preparation Time: | 10' | Servings: | 4 |

| Cooking Time: | 30' |

Ingredients

- ½ pounds boneless skinless chicken breasts
- 1 tablespoon fresh cilantro, chopped
- ¾ cup Lawry's Santa Fe Chili Marinated with Lime and Garlic, divided 1 package (10 ounces) torn romaine lettuce, approximately 8 cups
- 2 tablespoons milk
- 1 cup black beans, drained and rinsed
- ½ cup sour cream
- 1 cup drained canned whole kernel corn
- ¼ cup red onion, chopped
- 1 medium avocado, cut into chunks
- ½ cup Monterey Jack, shredded
- 1 medium tomato, cut into chunks

Directions

1. Place chicken in a large glass dish or re-sealable marinade plastic bag. Add approximately ½ cup of the Santa Fe marinade, turn several times until nicely coated
2. Refrigerate for 30 minutes or longer.
3. Removed the chicken from marinade; get rid of the leftover marinade. Grill the chicken until cooked through, for 6 to 7 minutes per side, over medium heat; brush with 2 tablespoons of the leftover marinade. Cut the chicken into thin slices.
4. Combine the sour cream together with milk, leftover marinade, and cilantro with wire whisk in a medium-sized bowl until smooth Arrange lettuce on large serving platter.
5. Top with the chicken, avocado, corn, beans, cheese, tomato, and onion.
6. Serve with tortilla chips and dressing. Enjoy

Nutrition: 676 Calories 86g Fat 67g Carbs 46g Protein

18. Quesadilla Explosion Salad

Preparation Time: 20'

Servings: 1

Cooking Time: 20'

Ingredients

- 1 vegetarian chicken patty
- 6 ounces bagged salad mix

For Chipotle Ranch Dressing:
- 1 cup 2% milk
- 1 packet ranch dressing mix
- 1 teaspoon chipotle peppers in adobo sauce
- 1 cup non-fat Greek yogurt

For Citrus Balsamic Vinaigrette
- 2 tablespoon balsamic vinegar
- ½ teaspoon orange zest
- 2 tablespoon Splenda
- ¼ cup orange juice
- A pinch of nutmeg
- For Sweet Potato Strips:
- ¼ medium sweet potato, washed, thinly sliced & cut into strips nonstick cooking spray
- ¼ teaspoon salt

For Cheese Quesadilla:
- 1 mission carb balance whole wheat fajita sized tortilla 1 ounce reduced-fat Colby Jack cheese, shredded

For Roasted Corn and Black Bean Salsa:
- 1 cup black beans, rinsed
- 2 ears of corn, roasted, kernels removed from cob
- ½ cup fresh cilantro, chopped
- 1 tablespoon lime juice, freshly squeezed
- ¼ red onion, chopped
- 1 jalapeno pepper, roasted, peeled, seeded, de-veined & chopped Salt to taste
- 1 red bell pepper, medium, roasted, peeled, seeded & chopped

Directions

For Sweet Potato Strips:
1. Preheat oven to 350 F. Lightly coat the strips with nonstick cooking spray and then dust them lightly with the salt. Place on a large-sized cookie sheet in a single layer & bake for 15 to 20 minutes. Don't forget to stir the strips & turn halfway during the baking process.
2. Set aside and let cool until ready to use.

For Roasted Corn Salsa:
3. Add corn together with peppers & black beans to a large bowl and then squeeze the lime juice on top; add salt to taste. Give the ingredients a good stir & add the fresh cilantro.

For Chipotle Ranch Dressing:
4. Add yogurt and milk to the ranch dressing mix. Stir in the chipotle & store in a refrigerator.
5. For Citrus Balsamic Vinaigrette:
6. Over low heat in a large saucepan; place the entire ingredients together & cook for a minute. Set aside and let cool, then refrigerate.

For Quesadilla:
7. Place the cheese on half of the tortilla & then fold over.
8. Lightly coat the tortilla with the nonstick cooking spray & then cook over medium-high heat in a large pan. Cook until the cheese is completely melted, for a minute per side. Cut into 4 wedges.
9. Prepare the veggie "chicken" patty as per the Directions mentioned on the package & then slice into thin strips.
10. Place approximately 6 ounces of the salad mix on the plate and then top with the "chicken" strips, black bean salsa, sweet potato strips & roasted corn.
11. Place the cut quesadilla around the edge of the plate and then drizzle the salad with the prepared dressings.

Nutrition: 245 Calories 59.8g Fat 67.3g Carbs 12.8g Protein

19. Caribbean Shrimp Salad

Preparation Time: 20'

Servings: 4

Cooking Time: 25'

Ingredients

- 8 cups baby spinach, fresh
- ¼ cup lime juice, freshly squeezed
- 2 tablespoons chili garlic sauce
- ½ teaspoon paprika
- 4 cups cooked shrimp
- 5 tablespoons seasoned rice vinegar, divided
- ½ teaspoon ground cumin
- 1 cup peeled mango, chopped
- ½ cup green onions, thinly sliced
- 2 garlic cloves, minced
- 1 cup radishes, julienne-cut
- ¼ cup peeled avocado, diced
- 2 tablespoons pumpkinseed kernels, unsalted 1 ½ tablespoons olive oil
- Dash of salt

Directions

1. In a large bowl; combine the cooked shrimp together with chili garlic sauce
2. & 2 tablespoons of vinegar; toss well. Cover & let chill for an hour.
3. Now, in a small bowl, combine the leftover vinegar together with garlic cloves, oil, lime juice, lime rind, ground cumin, paprika & salt, stirring well with a whisk.
4. Place 2 cups of spinach on each of 4 plates; top each serving with a cup of the prepared shrimp mixture. Arrange ¼ cup radishes, ¼ cup mango & 1 tablespoon of the avocado around the shrimp on each plate. Top each serving with approximately 1 ½ teaspoons of pumpkinseed kernels & 2 tablespoons of green onions. Drizzle each salad with approximately 2 tablespoons of the vinaigrette. Serve and enjoy.

Nutrition: 124 Calories 76.9g Fat 67.9g Carbs 45.8g Protein

20. Southwest Caesar Salad

Preparation Time: 10'

Servings: 6

Cooking Time: 20'

Ingredients

- 2 tablespoons mayonnaise
- ¼ teaspoon cayenne or ground red pepper
- 6 cups fresh romaine lettuce, washed
- 1/3 cup parmesan cheese, grated
- 1 cup croutons
- ½ of a red bell pepper, cut into thin strips
- 1 cup whole kernel corn, frozen & thawed
- ½ cup fresh cilantro, chopped
- 2 tablespoons green onion, chopped
- ¼ cup olive oil
- 2 tablespoon lime juice, freshly squeezed
- 1/8 teaspoon salt

Directions

1. Place onions together with mayo, ground red pepper, lime juice, and salt in a blender or food processor; cover & process until blended well. Slowly add the oil at the top using the feed tube & continue to process after each addition until blended well.
2. Toss the lettuce with the corn, croutons, bell peppers, cheese, and cilantro in a large bowl.
3. Add the mayo mixture; evenly toss until nicely coated. Serve immediately & enjoy.

Nutrition: 265 Calories 62g Fat 98g Carbs 47g Protein

21. Red Beans from Popeye's

Preparation Time: 20'

Servings: 10

Cooking Time: 40'

Ingredients

- 3 14-ounce cans red beans
- ¾ pounds smoked ham hock
- 1¼ cups water
- ½ teaspoon onion powder
- ½ teaspoon garlic salt
- ¼ teaspoon red pepper flakes
- ½ teaspoon salt
- 3 tablespoons lard
- Steamed long-grain rice

Directions

1. Add 2 canned red beans, ham hock, and water to the pot. Cook on medium heat and let simmer for about 1 hour.
2. Remove from heat and wait until the meat is cool enough to handle. Then remove meat from the bone.
3. In a food processor, add meat, cooked red beans and water mixture, onion powder, garlic salt, red pepper, salt, and lard. Pulse for 4 seconds. You want the beans to be cut, and the liquid thickened. Drain the remaining 1 can red beans and add to the food processor. Pulse for only 1 or 2 seconds.
4. Remove ingredients from the food processor and transfer to the pot from earlier.
5. Cook on low heat, stirring frequently until mixture is heated through. Serve over steamed rice.

Nutrition: 445 Calories 12g Fat 67g Carbs 9g Fibers

22. Café Rio's Sweet Pork Barbacoa Salad

Preparation Time: 10'

Servings: 8

Cooking Time: 8'

Ingredients

- 3 pounds pork loin
- Garlic salt, to taste
- 1 can root beer
- ¼ cup water
- ¾ cup brown sugar
- 1 10-ounce can red enchilada sauce
- 1 4-ounce can green chilies
- ½ teaspoon chili powder
- 8 large burrito size tortillas
- 1½ serving Cilantro Lime Rice
- 1 can black beans, drained and heated
- 2 heads Romaine lettuce, shredded
- 1½ cups tortilla strips
- 1 cup Queso Fresco cheese
- 2 limes, cut in wedges
- ¼ cup cilantro

Dressing:
- ½ packet Hidden Valley Ranch Dressing Mix 1 cup mayonnaise
- ½ cup milk
- ½ cup cilantro leaves
- ¼ cup salsa Verde
- ½ jalapeno pepper, deseeded
- 1 plump clove garlic
- 2 tablespoons fresh lime juice

Directions

1. Sprinkle garlic salt on pork. Put in the slow cooker with the flat side facing down.
2. Add ¼ cup root beer and water. Cover and cook on low setting for 6 hours.
3. To prepare sauce, add the rest of the root beer, brown sugar, enchilada sauce, green chilies, and chili powder in a blender. Blend until smooth.
4. Remove meat from slow cooker then transfer onto the cutting board. Shred, discarding juices and fat. Return shredded pork to slow cooker with the sauce.
5. Cook on low setting for another 2 hours. When there is only about 15 to 20
6. minutes left to cook, remove the lid to thicken the sauce.
7. To prepare the dressing, mix all dressing ingredients in a blender. Puree until smooth. Then, transfer to the refrigerator and allow to chill for at least 1 hour.
8. To assemble the salad, layer tortilla, rice, beans, pork, lettuce, tortilla strips, cheese, and dressing in a bowl. Serve with a lime wedge and cilantro leaves.

Nutrition: 756 Calories 28g Fat 91g Carbs 7g Fibers

23. Almond Crusted Salmon Salad

Preparation Time: 15'

Servings: 4

Cooking Time: 30'

Ingredients

- ¼ cup olive oil
- 4 (4-ounce) portions salmon
- ½ teaspoon kosher salt
- 1/8 teaspoon ground black pepper
- 2 tablespoons garlic aioli (bottled is fine)
- ½ cup chopped and ground almonds for crust
- 10 ounces kale, chopped
- ¼ cup lemon dressing of choice
- 2 avocados, peeled, pitted, and cut into ½-inch pieces 2 cups cooked quinoa
- 1 cup brussels sprouts, sliced
- 2 ounces arugula
- ½ cup dried cranberries
- 1 cup balsamic vinaigrette
- 24 thin radish slices
- Lemon zest

Directions

1. In a large skillet, heat the olive oil over medium-high heat. Sprinkle the salmon with salt and pepper to season. When the skillet is hot, add the fish fillets and cook for about 3 minutes on each side or until it flakes easily with a fork. Top the salmon with garlic aioli and sprinkle with nuts.
2. Meanwhile, combine all the salad ingredients, including the quinoa, in a bowl, and toss with the dressing.
3. Serve the salad with a fish fillet on top of greens and sprinkle with radishes and lemon zest.

Nutrition: 243 Calories 45g Fat 23g Carbs 52g Protein

24. Deep Fried Pickles from Texas Roadhouse

Preparation Time: 10'

Servings: 4

Cooking Time: 10'

Ingredients

- Vegetable oil, for deep frying
- ¼ cup flour
- 1¼ teaspoons Cajun seasoning, divided
- ¼ teaspoon oregano
- ¼ teaspoon basil
- 1/8 teaspoon cayenne pepper
- Kosher salt
- 2 cups dill pickles, drained and sliced
- ¼ cup mayonnaise
- 1 tablespoon horseradish
- 1 tablespoon ketchup

Directions

1. Preheat about 1½ inches oil to 375°F in a large pot.
2. In a separate bowl, make the coating by combining flour, 1 teaspoon Cajun seasoning, oregano, basil, cayenne pepper, and Kosher salt.
3. Dredge pickle slices in flour mixture. Lightly shake to remove any excess, then carefully lower into the hot oil. Work in batches so as not to overcrowd the pot. Deep fry for about 2 minutes or until lightly brown.
4. Using a slotted spoon, transfer pickles to a plate lined with paper towels to drain.
5. While pickles drain and cool, add mayonnaise, horseradish, ketchup, and remaining Cajun seasoning in a bowl. Mix well. Serve immediately with dip on the side.

Nutrition: 296 Calories 28g Total fat 12g Carbs 1g Protein

25. Chili's Chili

Preparation Time: 10'

Servings: 8

Cooking Time: 1 h 10'

Ingredients

For Chili:
- 4 pounds ground chuck - ground for chili
- 1 ½ cups yellow onions, chopped
- 16 ounces tomato sauce
- 1 tablespoon cooking oil
- 3 ¼ plus 1 cups water
- 1 tablespoon masa harina

For Chili Spice Blend:
- 1 tablespoon paprika
- ½ cup chili powder
- 1 teaspoon ground black pepper
- 1/8 cup ground cumin
- 1 teaspoon cayenne pepper or to taste
- 1/8 cup salt
- 1 teaspoon garlic powder

Directions

1. Combine the entire chili spice ingredients together in a small bowl; continue to combine until thoroughly mixed.
2. Now, over moderate heat in a 6-quart stock pot; place & cook the meat until browned; drain. In the meantime, combine the chili spice mix together with tomato sauce & 3 ¼ cups of water in the bowl; give the ingredients a good stir until blended well.
3. Add the chili seasoning liquid to the browned meat; give it a good stir & bring the mixture to a boil over moderate heat.
4. Over medium heat in a large skillet; heat 1 tablespoon of the cooking oil & sauté the onions until translucent, for a couple of minutes. Add the sautéed onions to the chili.
5. Decrease the heat to low & let simmer for an hour, stirring after every 10 to 15 minutes. Combine the masa harina with the leftover water in a separate bowl; mix well. Add to the chili stock pot & cook for 10 more minutes

Nutrition: 143 Calories 51g Fat 63.6g Carbs 13.8g Protein

26. Ham Salad

Preparation Time: 5'

Servings: 2-3

Cooking Time: 5'

Ingredients

- 3 cups Head of Lettuce, shredded
- 200 g baby spinach
- 1/2 cup Shredded Provolone Cheese
- 6 slices Black Forest Ham, cut into strips
- 1/4 cup pickled jalapeno peppers, sliced
- 1/4 cup Black olives
- 1 whole Tomato, thinly sliced or grape tomatoes 1/3 cup
- 1/4 cup ranch dressing or dressing of your choice

Directions

1. Mix and toss all ingredients in a bowl and serve immediately

Nutrition: 110 Calories 2.5g Fat 5g Fiber 12g Carbs 12g Protein

27. Italian B.M.T. ® Salad

Preparation Time: 15'

Servings: 2-3

Cooking Time: 0'

Ingredients

- 3 cups Head of Lettuce, shredded
- 200 g baby spinach
- 1/2 cup Shredded Provolone Cheese
- 4 slices Salami Meat, cut into strips
- 4 slices Black Forest Ham, cut into strips
- 6 pieces Pepperoni
- 1/4 cup Black olives
- 1/4 cup Banana Peppers, sliced
- ¼ cup Green Pepper sliced thinly
- 1 whole Tomato
- 1/4 cup any dressing of your choice

Directions

1. Mix and toss all ingredients in a bowl and serve immediately!

Nutrition: 410 Calories 42g Fat 3g Fiber 10g Carbs 12g Protein

28. Roasted Chicken Salad

Preparation Time: 6H or overnight	**Servings:** 4-5
Cooking Time: 20-30'	

Ingredients

For grilled chicken
- 2 chicken breasts, deboned
- 1 tsp salt
- 1 tbsp Italian seasoning
- 1 tbsp lemon juice
- ½ tsp msg
- ¼ tsp garlic powder
- ½ tsp onion powder
- ½ tsp black pepper

For Dressing
- 1/3 cup plain nonfat yogurt
- 1 teaspoon sugar
- 4 teaspoons lemon juice
- 4 tablespoons light mayonnaise
- Salt and pepper

For assembly
- 3 cups lettuce
- ½ cup diced celery
- 300 g baby spinach
- ½ cup diced cucumber
- 1 cup chopped red apples
- ¼ cup dried cranberries or cherries
- ¼ cup golden raisins or white grapes

Directions

1. Prepare the chicken breast for marinating; pound each breast until even in thickness. Combine all ingredients remaining in a bowl and put in chicken breast pieces. Marinate overnight or a minimum of 6 hrs. Once the margination is done, put the chicken breast in a pan and roast in the oven for about 20-30 minutes, brushing it with the excess marinade every now and then. While waiting, prepare the dressing. Mix all ingredients under the dressing in a small bowl and chill for 15 minutes. Slices all the needed toppings and set aside. When the chicken is cooked, cut into cubes or strips.
2. Toss everything in a large bowl and serve immediately.

Nutrition: 140 Calories 2.5g Fat 4g Fiber 11g Carbs 19g Protein

29. Roast Beef Salad

Preparation Time: 5'

Servings: 4-5

Cooking Time: 10'

Ingredients

- 4 thinly sliced roast beef
- 3 cups lettuce
- ½ cup diced celery
- 300 g baby spinach
- ½ cup diced cucumber
- ¼ cup dried cranberries or cherries
- 1/4 cup Black olives
- 1/4 cup Banana Peppers, sliced
- ¼ cup Green Pepper sliced thinly
- 1 whole Tomato, thinly sliced or grape tomatoes 1/3 cup
- 1/4 cup any dressing of your choice

Directions

1. Mix and toss all ingredients in a bowl and serve immediately!

Nutrition: 150 Calories 3.5g Fat 6g Fiber 14g Carbs 21g Protein

30. Steak & Cheese Salad

| Preparation Time: | 30-40' | | Servings: | 3-4 |

| Cooking Time: | 15-20' |

Ingredients

- 2 cloves garlic chopped
- 1/8 cup Dijon mustard
- 1/8 cup extra-virgin olive oil
- ¼ cup balsamic vinegar
- ½ tsp. Black pepper
- 1tsp.salt
- 1 1/2 lb. flank steak
- 3 cups Head of Lettuce, shredded
- 200 g baby spinach
- 1/2 cup cheese sauce
- 1/4 cup Black olives
- 1/4 cup jalapeno peppers, sliced
- ¼ cup Green Bell pepper, sliced thinly
- 1 whole Tomato, thinly sliced or grape tomatoes 1/3 cup

Directions

1. In a bowl, mix the balsamic vinegar and mustard. Whisk in olive oil and garlic, then season with pepper and salt. Put in steak and marinate for 30 minutes or more. While waiting, prepare other ingredients for assembly of the salad.
2. After marinating, grill the steak according to your preferred doneness and let it rest before slicing. Mix all ingredients in a bowl and top off with cheese sauce.

Nutrition: 180 Calories 8g Fat 4g Fiber 14g Carbs 17g Protein

31. Subway Club ® Salad

Preparation Time: 10'

Servings: 3-4

Cooking Time: 10'

Ingredients

- 2 pcs turkey breast, cut into strips
- 2 pcs lean roast beef, cut into strips
- 2 slices Black Forest ham, cut into strips
- 400g shredded lettuce
- 1/3 cup halved cherry tomatoes
- 1 whole chopped avocado
- 1/3 cup croutons
- 2 pcs hard-boiled eggs, quartered
- ½ cup Cucumber, diced
- For the dressing:
- ¼ cup mayonnaise
- ¼ cup yellow mustard
- 1 tbsp vinegar
- Salt and pepper

Directions

1. Make the dressing by mixing all the ingredients in a small bowl. Mix and toss everything in a bowl and serve immediately.

Nutrition: 140 Calories 3.5g Fat 4g Fiber 12g Carbs 19g Protein

32. Subway Melt ® Salad

Preparation Time: 5'

Servings: 3-4

Cooking Time: 10'

Ingredients

- 2 pcs turkey breast, cut into strips
- 4 pcs smoked bacon, cooked until crisp and crumbled
- 2 slices Black Forest ham, cut into strips
- 400g shredded lettuce
- 1/3 cup halved cherry tomatoes
- ¼ cup jalapeno peppers
- 5 pieces black olives, sliced
- 1/3 cup croutons
- 2 pcs hard-boiled eggs, quartered
- ½ cup shredded provolone cheese
- ½ cup Cucumber, diced
- 1/3 cup ranch dressing or any dressing of your choice

Directions

1. Mix and toss everything in a bowl and serve immediately.

Nutrition: 150 Calories 4.1g Fat 4g Fiber 15g Carbs 21g Protein

33. Chicken Teriyaki Salad

Preparation Time: 5'

Servings: 4-5

Cooking Time: 5'

Ingredients

- 2 boneless, skinless chicken breasts
- ½ cup store-bought teriyaki marinade

For assembly
- 8 slices of cucumber
- 1/4 cup Black olives
- 1/4 cup Banana Peppers, sliced
- ¼ cup Green Pepper sliced thinly
- ½ red onion thinly sliced
- 1 whole Tomato, thinly sliced or grape tomatoes 1/3 cup
- 300g lettuce
- 200 g baby spinach
- Sweet Onion Sauce
- 1 tablespoon red wine vinegar
- 1/3 cup light corn syrup
- 1 tablespoon white vinegar
- 2 tablespoon minced white onion
- 2 teaspoon balsamic vinegar
- ½ tsp garlic powder
- 1/4 teaspoon salt
- 4 teaspoon brown sugar
- ½ teaspoon lemon juice
- 1/8 tsp black pepper
- 1/4 teaspoon poppy seeds

Directions

1. Put teriyaki marinade and chicken breast in a bowl and marinate for at least 30 minutes. While the chicken is marinating, prepare the sweet onion sauce by combining everything in a pan and heat them until it boils. Cool down. Slice all vegetables for the salad and set aside. Grill or panfry chicken and brush with marinade once in a while. Once cooked, slice into strips or cubes. Mix and toss everything in a bowl and serve immediately.

Nutrition: 240 Calories 3g Fat 4g Fiber 35g Carbs 20g Protein

34. Tuna Salad

Preparation Time: 10'

Servings: 4-5

Cooking Time: 15'

Ingredients

For tuna mixture
- 1 can tuna (drained)
- 4 tablespoons mayonnaise
- 2 teaspoon lemon juice
- salt and pepper to taste

For assembly:
- 8 slices of cucumber
- 1/4 cup Black olives
- 1/4 cup Banana Peppers, sliced
- ¼ cup Green Pepper sliced thinly
- ½ red onion thinly sliced
- 1 whole Tomato, thinly sliced or grape tomatoes 1/3 cup
- 300g lettuce
- 200 g baby spinach

Directions

1. Mix tuna, mayo, lemon juice, salt and pepper, and chill. While waiting, prepare all remaining ingredients for assembly. Mix and toss everything in a bowl and serve immediately.

Nutrition: 280 Calories 12g Fat 1g Fiber 24g Carbs 10g Protein

35. Turkey Salad

Preparation Time: 5'

Servings: 3-4

Cooking Time: 0

Ingredients

- 4 slices Smoked Turkey Breast, cut into strips
- 2 pcs American Cheese, shredded
- 5 slices of cucumber
- 1/8 cup Black olives
- ¼ cup Green Pepper sliced thinly
- ¼ red onion thinly sliced
- 1 whole Tomato, thinly sliced or grape tomatoes 1/3 cup
- 300g lettuce
- 200 g baby spinach
- 1/3 cup dressing of your choice

Directions

1. Mix and toss everything in a bowl and serve immediately

Nutrition: 110 Calories 2g Fat 4g Fiber 12g Carbs 12g Protein

Chapter 2

Old and Modern Sweet and Savory Snack Recipes

36. Roadhouse Mashed Potatoes

Preparation Time: 20'

Servings: 6

Cooking Time: 30'

Ingredients

- ¼ cup Parmesan cheese, grated
- 1 whole garlic bulb
- ¼ cup sour cream
- 4 medium potatoes, peeled & quartered
- ¼ cup each of softened butter & 2% milk
- 1 teaspoon plus 1 tablespoon olive oil, divided
- ¼ teaspoon pepper
- 1 medium white onion, chopped
- ½ teaspoon salt

Directions

1. Preheat the oven to 425 degrees. Cut off the papery outer skin from the garlic bulb; ensure that you don't separate the cloves or peel them. Remove the top from the garlic bulb, exposing individual cloves. Brush cut cloves with approximately 1 teaspoon of oil, then wrap in foil. Bake in the preheated oven for 30 to 35 minutes until cloves are soft.
2. Meanwhile, cook the leftover oil over low heat. Once done, add & cook the chopped onion for 15 to 20 minutes, until golden brown, stirring every now and then. Transfer to a food processor. Process on high until blended well; set aside.
3. Put the potatoes in a large saucepan and cover them with water. Bring to a boil. Once done, decrease the heat; cook for 15 to 20 minutes, until tender, uncovered. Drain; return to the pan. Squeeze the softened garlic over the potatoes; add butter, cheese, sour cream, milk, onion, pepper, and salt. Beat until mashed. Serve and enjoy.

Nutrition: 220 calories 15g total fats 3g protein

37. Sweet Potatoes with Marshmallows and Caramel Sauce

Preparation Time: 40'

Servings: 10'

Cooking Time: 30'

Ingredients

- ½ cup corn syrup
- 6 medium sweet potatoes, peeled & cut into 1" chunks
- ½ teaspoon ground cinnamon
- ¼ cup whole milk
- 2 tablespoons butter
- ½ cup brown sugar, packed
- Marshmallows on top
- ½ to 1 teaspoon salt

Directions

1. Put sweet potatoes in a Dutch oven; add water and ensure that the sweet potatoes are nicely covered. Bring to a boil. Once done, decrease the heat; cover & let simmer for 20 minutes.
2. Drain & transfer to a lightly greased 13x9" baking dish. Bake for 12 to 15 minutes, at 325 F, uncovered.
3. In the meantime, combine the leftover ingredients (except the marshmallows) together in a small saucepan. Bring to a boil; pour the mixture on top of the sweet potatoes. Bake until glazed, for 10 to15 more minutes, basting frequently. Just before serving, throw some marshmallows on top. Enjoy.

Nutrition: 180 calories 12g total fats 4g protein

38. Sautéed Mushrooms

Preparation Time: 20'

Servings: 6

Cooking Time: 20'

Ingredients

- 1 teaspoon garlic, chopped
- 1 tablespoon butter
- 1 cup cleaned Portobello mushrooms, sliced
- 1 tablespoon thyme leaves, chopped
- 1/8 cup vegetable oil
- Freshly ground black pepper & salt to taste

Directions

1. Warm up the oil over high heat in a large skillet until hot & smoky. Add the garlic; cook until turn fragrant, toss it constantly, and ensure that the garlic doesn't burn. Add the mushrooms; toss until mushrooms are caramelized and turn golden brown. Remove from the heat. Add butter and thyme; season with pepper and salt, to taste. Serve immediately & enjoy.

Nutrition: 191 calories 13g total fats 5g protein

39. Ham and Cheese Empanadas

Preparation Time: 5'

Servings: 6

Cooking Time: 15'

Ingredients

- 12 cooked ham feta
- 400 g mozzarella cheese
- 12 empanada tapas
- Dried oregano
- Ground chili pepper
- 1 beaten egg

Directions

1. Cut the mozzarella cheese into 12 bars of approximately 30-35 g each. Pass the bars with oregano and floor chili pepper and area them in the center of each ham feta. Wrap the cheese with the ham, forming a bundle, and reserve. This is so that the cheese does no longer explode in the oven or while you're frying them.
2. Stretch the dough of the empanadas a touch so that they're oval and locate the applications of ham and cheese in the center of each one in all them.
3. Close the middle and locate a finger inside to push the ham even as persevering with to close the sides. This is so that the ham does not complicate your existence at the time of creating the repulse. Make the traditional repulgue and forestalls placed them in an appropriate greased baking sheet with oil. Paint the pies ham and cheese with crushed egg if desired and takes a warm oven till their golden brown.
4. If you want to fry ham and cheese empanadas, consider that the oil must be at 150-160 ° C, because if it had been hotter, they would be cooked on the outside, and inside, the cheese could no longer melt. Fry them for about 3 minutes. Remove the patties fried ham and cheese with a slotted spoon and depart them on paper towels to cast off extra oil.

Nutrition: 188 calories 16g total fats 11g protein

40. Roadhouse Green Beans

Preparation Time: 10'

Servings: 8

Cooking Time: 20'

Ingredients

- 2 cans green beans (16 ounces), drained
- 1 tablespoon sugar
- 4 ounces bacon, diced (raw) or 4 ounces ham (cooked)
- 2 cups water
- 4 ounces onions, diced
- ½ teaspoon pepper

Directions

1. Thoroughly drain green beans using a colander; set aside. Combine pepper with sugar & water until incorporated well; set aside. Preheat your cooking pan over medium-high heat.
2. Dice the cooked ham into equal size pieces using a cutting board and a knife. Place the diced onions and ham into the preheated cooking pan. Continue to stir the onions and ham using the large spoon until the onions are tender and the ham is lightly brown.
3. Once done, add the beans and liquid mixture. Using the rubber spatula, give the mixture a good stir until incorporated well. Let the mixture boil, then lower the heat to simmer. Serve the beans as soon as you are ready and enjoy.

Nutrition: 221 calories 16g total fats 4g protein

41. Roadhouse Cheese Fries

Preparation Time: 20'

Servings: 4

Cooking Time: 30'

Ingredients

- 6 -8 slices bacon, enough to make ½ cup once cooked
- 4 cups steak-style French fries, frozen
- ¼ teaspoon onion powder
- 2 cups sharp cheddar cheese, grated
- Oil for frying
- ¼ teaspoon each of garlic salt & seasoning salt

Directions

1. Preheat your oven to 450 F. Cook the bacon over medium-high heat in a medium-sized frying pan. Take out the bacon when crisp & place it on a paper towel to drain.
2. Pour the bacon grease into a bowl & let slightly cool. Add onion powder, seasoned salt, and garlic salt to the grease; combine well and set aside. Assemble the fries on a greased baking sheet & bake in the preheated oven until turn slightly golden, for 10 to 15 minutes.
3. Set your oven to broil. Brush the bacon oil with the seasoning mix onto each fry. Place fries in an oven-safe bowl. Spread the cheddar cheese on top of the fries. Crumble bacon slices and then sprinkle on top of the cheese.
4. Place dish in the oven until the cheese is bubbly, for 3 to 5 minutes. Remove from the oven & let sit for a couple of minutes, then serve.

Nutrition: 188 calories 11 total fats 4g protein

42. Dinner Rolls

Preparation Time: 1 H

Servings: 4

Cooking Time: 15'

Ingredients

For Rolls:
- 2 ¼ teaspoon or 1 packet active dry yeast
- 1 large egg, at room temperature
- 1 ¼ cup milk
- 4 tablespoons melted butter, separated
- ¼ cup honey
- 4 cups flour
- 1 teaspoon salt

For Texas Roadhouse Butter:
- ¼ cup powdered sugar
- 1 stick salted butter, at room temperature for an hour
- ¾ teaspoon cinnamon
- 1 ½ tablespoons honey

Directions

1. For Texas Roadhouse Butter
2. Using an electric mixer, combine the entire Roadhouse butter ingredients together until smooth & creamy. Refrigerate until ready to use.
3. For Rolls:
4. Bring the milk to a boil over moderate heat. Once done, remove the pan from heat & set aside at room temperature until lukewarm.
5. Now, combine the milk with honey & yeast in a small bowl until combined well. Let sit for a couple of minutes. Combine 2 cups of flour with milk mixture, egg & 3 tablespoons of butter in a large bowl. Slowly mix until smooth. Slowly add the leftover flour & continue to mix until dough-like consistency is achieved.
6. Add salt & continue to mix for 6 to 8 more minutes. Drop the dough onto a floured surface; knead for a couple of minutes more. Grease the large bowl with the cooking spray & drop the dough inside. Using a plastic wrap, cover the bowl & let rise in a warm place for an hour.
7. Coat 2 cookie sheets lightly with the vegetable oil. Punch the dough down & roll it out on a flat, floured surface until it's approximately ½" thick. Fold it in half & gently seal. Evenly cut the dough into 24 squares & arrange them on the prepared cookie sheets. Using a plastic wrap, cover & let them rise until almost doubled in size, for 35 to 40 minutes.
8. Preheat your oven to 350 F in advance & bake until the top is a light golden brown, for 12 to 15 minutes. Heat the leftover tablespoon of butter until melted and then brush the top of the rolls.
9. Serve with Texas Roadhouse Butter and enjoy.

Nutrition: 210 calories 14g total fats 5g protein

43. Texas Red Chili

Preparation Time: 2'

Servings: 4

Cooking Time: 5'

Ingredients

- 2 ½ pounds boneless beef chuck, well-trimmed & cut into ¾" cubes
- 1 ½ teaspoons ground cumin seed
- 2 ounces pasilla chilis
- 1/3 cup onion, finely chopped
- 3 large garlic cloves, minced
- 2 ¼ cups water, plus more as needed
- Sour cream
- 1 tablespoon firmly packed dark brown sugar, plus more as needed
- 2 tablespoons masa harina (corn tortilla flour)
- 1 ½ tablespoons distilled white vinegar, plus more as needed
- 2 cups canned low-sodium beef broth or beef stock, plus more as required
- Lime wedges
- ½ teaspoon freshly ground black pepper
- 5 tablespoons vegetable oil, lard or rendered beef suet
- Kosher salt to taste

Directions

1. Over medium-low heat in a straight-sided large skillet; gently toast the chilies for 2 to 3 minutes per side, until fragrant. Keep an eye on them and don't let them burn. Place the chilies in a large bowl & cover them with very hot water; let soak for 15 to 45 minutes, until soft, turning a couple of times during the soaking process.
2. Drain the chilies; split them & remove the seeds and stems. Place the chilies in a blender & then add the black pepper, cumin, ¼ cup water, and 1 tablespoon salt. Purée the mixture until a smooth, slightly fluid paste forms; feel free to add more of water as required and scrape down the sides of your blender jar occasionally. Set aside until ready to use.
3. Place the skillet over medium-high heat again & heat 2 tablespoons of lard until melted. When it starts to smoke, swirl to coat the bottom of your skillet & add half of the beef. Lightly brown on at least two sides, for 2 to 3 minutes on each side. If the meat threatens to burn, immediately decrease the heat. Transfer to a bowl & repeat with 2 more tablespoons of lard & the leftover beef. Reserve.
4. Let the skillet to slightly cool & place it over medium-low heat. Heat the leftover lard in the same skillet. Once melted, immediately add the garlic and onion; gently cook for 3 to 4 minutes, stirring every now and then. Add the stock & the leftover water; slowly whisk in the masa harina to avoid lumps. Stir in the reserved chili paste, scraping the bottom of your skillet using a spatula to loosen any browned bits. Place the reserved beef (along with any accumulated juices) & bring to a simmer over high heat. Once done, decrease the heat to maintain the barest possible simmer & continue to cook for 2 hours, until 1 ½ to 2 cups of thickened but still liquid sauce surrounds the cubes of meat & the meat is tender but still somewhat firm, stirring occasionally.
5. Thoroughly stir in the vinegar & brown sugar; add more salt to taste; let simmer gently for 10 more minutes. Switch it off and set aside for 30 minutes. If the mixture appears to be too dry, feel free to stir in the additional water or broth. Alternatively, let it simmer a couple of more minutes, if the mixture appears to be a bit loose & wet. Alter the balance of flavors with a bit of additional vinegar, sugar, or salt, if desired.
6. Gently reheat & serve in separate bowls with a dollop of sour cream on top & a fresh lime wedge on the side.

Nutrition: 218 calories 13g total fats 4g protein

44. Boneless Buffalo Wings

Preparation Time: 25'

Servings: 2 dozen

Cooking Time: 2H 15'

Ingredients

- 1 cup low-sodium soy sauce
- ½ teaspoon pepper
- 2 teaspoons grated orange zest
- 3 pounds boneless chicken wings
- 2 garlic cloves, minced
- 2/3 cup sugar
- 3 teaspoons chili powder
- ¾ teaspoon each of cayenne pepper & hot pepper sauce
- 2 teaspoons salt
- For Blue Cheese Dip:
- ½ cup blue cheese salad dressing
- 2 teaspoons Italian salad dressing mix
- 1 cup mayonnaise
- ☐ cup buttermilk

Directions

1. Combine the orange zest, sugar, soy sauce, pepper, garlic, and salt in a small bowl. Pour half of the marinade into a large re-sealable plastic bag. Mix in the chicken pieces; seal the bag & turn the pieces several times until nicely coated. Refrigerate for an hour. Using a plastic wrap, cover the leftover marinade & refrigerate.
2. Drain & discard the marinade. Transfer the chicken to a lightly greased 13x9" baking dish. Cover & bake until juices of the chicken run clear, for 1 ½ hours, at 325 F.
3. Transfer the cooked chicken to a greased 15x10x1" baking pan using a pair of tongs. Combine the pepper sauce together with chili powder, cayenne & reserved marinade in a small bowl. Drizzle on top of the chicken.
4. Bake for 30 minutes, uncovered, turning once. Whisk the entire dipping ingredients together in a small bowl. Serve with the cooked wings and enjoy.

Nutrition: 211 calories 12g total fats 5.3g protein

45. Tater Skins

Preparation Time: 5'

Servings: 8

Cooking Time: 35'

Ingredients

- 4 large baking potatoes, baked
- ¼ teaspoon garlic powder
- 4 green onions, sliced
- 1 tablespoon Parmesan cheese, grated
- 1/8 teaspoon pepper
- 8 bacon strips, cooked & crumbled
- ½ cup sour cream
- 1 ½ cups cheddar cheese, shredded
- ¼ teaspoon paprika
- 3 tablespoons canola oil
- ½ teaspoon salt

Directions

1. Preheat the oven to 475 degrees. Slice the potatoes lengthwise in half; scoop the pulp out; leaving approximately ¼" shell. Place the potato skins on a lightly greased baking sheet.
2. Combine oil with the cheese, pepper, paprika, garlic powder & salt; mix well and then brush over the skins on both sides.
3. Bake both sides until turn crisp. Sprinkle the cheddar cheese & bacon inside the skins. Bake until the cheese is completely melted. Top with onions and sour cream. Serve immediately and enjoy.

Nutrition: 221 calories 16g total fats 5g protein

46. Fried Pickles

Preparation Time: 15'

Servings: 8

Cooking Time: 25'

Ingredients

- ½ teaspoon garlic powder
- 32 dill pickle slices
- ½ cup all-purpose flour
- 2 large eggs, lightly beaten
- ½ teaspoon cayenne pepper
- 2 tablespoons dill pickle juice
- ½ cup Japanese (panko) breadcrumbs
- 1 tablespoon fresh dill, snipped
- ½ teaspoon salt

Directions

1. Preheat the oven to 500 degrees. Place the pickles to stand on a paper towel until the liquid is almost absorbed.
2. In the meantime, blend the flour with salt in a shallow bowl. Whisk the eggs together with pickle juice, garlic powder, and cayenne in a separate shallow bowl. Combine the dill with panko in a third shallow bowl.
3. Dip the pickles first into the flour mixture (ensure both sides are nicely coated); shake off any excess, then dip into the egg mixture and finally into the crumb mixture, patting to help the coating to adhere. Transfer to a lightly greased wire rack in a rimmed baking sheet.
4. Bake until turn golden brown & crispy. Serve immediately & enjoy.

Nutrition: 218 calories 14g total fats 3g protein

47. Rattlesnake Bites

Preparation Time: 15'

Servings: 6 dozen

Cooking Time: 35'

Ingredients

- 2 teaspoons baking powder
- 1 cup plus 3 tablespoons all-purpose flour
- 2 cups cornmeal
- 1 ½ teaspoons sugar
- ½ teaspoon baking soda
- 1 large egg
- 2/3 cup water
- 1 small green pepper, chopped
- ½ cup butter, melted
- 2 jalapeno peppers, seeded & chopped
- ½ cup buttermilk
- 1 cup onion, grated
- Oil for deep-fat frying
- 1 teaspoon salt

Directions

1. Combine the flour together with cornmeal, sugar, baking powder, baking soda, and salt in a large bowl. Whisk the egg with water, butter, and buttermilk in a separate bowl. Stir in the jalapenos, onion & green pepper. Stir the mixture into the dry ingredients until just moistened.
2. Now, over moderate heat in a deep-fat fryer or an electric skillet; heat the oil until hot. Using teaspoonfuls, drop the batter carefully into the hot oil, a few at a time. Fry until both sides turn golden brown. Place them on paper towels to drain. Serve warm and enjoy.

Nutrition: 210 calories 10g total fats 4.3g protein

48. Cactus Blossom

Preparation Time: 25'

Servings: 8

Cooking Time: 40'

Ingredients

- 3 tablespoons dry breadcrumbs
- 1 tablespoon butter, melted
- 2 large sweet onions
- ¼ teaspoon each of pepper & salt
- 2 teaspoons Dijon mustard
- For Sauce:
- ¼ cup each of sour cream & mayonnaise, fat-free
- 1 ½ teaspoons dried minced onion
- ¼ teaspoon each of garlic powder & dill weed

Directions

1. Slice ½" off the top of the onions using a sharp knife; peel the onions. Cut each into 16 wedges to within ½" of the root end. Place each onion on a double thickness of heavy-duty foil (approximately 12" square). Fold the foil around onions & tightly seal. Place in an ungreased 11x7" baking dish. Bake for 20 minutes at 425 F, uncovered.
2. Combine the butter with mustard in a small bowl. Carefully open the foil; fold the foil around the onions. Brush the butter mixture on top of the onions; sprinkle with breadcrumbs, pepper, and salt.
3. Bake until crisp-tender, for 20 to 22 more minutes. In the meantime, combine the entire sauce ingredients together in a small bowl. Serve with the onions.

Nutrition: 219 calories 14g total fats 5g protein

49. Crispy Cheesy Chips

Preparation Time: 10'

Servings: 8

Cooking Time: 10'

Ingredients

- 1 cup whey protein isolate
- 4 cups shredded mozzarella cheese

Directions

1. Take a medium heatproof bowl, place cheese in it, and then microwave for 1 minute until cheese melts.
2. Remove the bowl from the oven and immediately stir in whey protein until well combined and the dough comes together.
3. Spread a sheet of parchment on working space, place half of the dough on it, and then cover it with the parchment sheet of the same size.
4. Shape the dough into a thin rectangle by using hands and rolling pin and then cut out triangles by using a pizza cutter.
5. Repeat with the remaining dough to make more chips. Transfer the cheese triangles onto two large baking sheets, leaving some space between them, and then bake for 8 to 10 minutes until nicely browned.
6. When done, let the chips cool for 5 minutes and then serve with a dip.

Nutrition: 164 Calories 0.4g Fats 36.8g Protein

50. Brined Chicken Bites

Preparation Time: 10'

Servings: 4

Cooking Time: 20'

Ingredients

- 1-pound chicken breast
- ½ teaspoon salt
- 2 cups pickle juice
- Avocado oil, as needed for frying

For the Coating:
- 1 tablespoon baking powder
- ½ teaspoon garlic powder
- ½ teaspoon salt
- 1 tablespoon erythritol sweetener
- ½ teaspoon ground black pepper
- ½ teaspoon paprika
- ½ cup whey protein powder

Directions

1. Cut the chicken into 1-inch pieces, place them in a large plastic bag, add salt, pour in pickle juice, and then seal the bag.
2. Turn it upside down to coat the chicken pieces and then let marinate for a minimum of 30 minutes in the refrigerator.
3. Then remove chicken from the refrigerator, let it rest at room temperature for 25 minutes, drain it well, and pat dry with paper towels.
4. Cook the chicken and for this, take a large pot, place it over medium-low heat, pour in oil until the pot has half-full, and then bring it to 350 degrees F.
5. Meanwhile, prepare the coating and for this, take a medium bowl, place all of its ingredients in it and then stir until mixed.
6. Dredge a chicken piece into the coating mixture until thoroughly covered, arrange it onto a baking sheet lined with parchment paper and repeat with the remaining pieces.
7. Drop the prepared chicken pieces into the oil, fry for 6 minutes until thoroughly cooked, and then transfer to a plate lined with paper towels. Repeat with the remaining chicken pieces and then serve.

Nutrition: 284 Calories 17g Fats 34g Protein 1g Carb

51. Bloomin' Onion

Preparation Time: 15'

Servings: 4

Cooking Time: 5'

Ingredients

- 1 large sweet onion
- ½ cup coconut flour
- ½ tablespoon seasoning salt
- ½ teaspoon ground black pepper
- ½ teaspoon cayenne
- ½ tablespoon paprika
- 4 tablespoons heavy whipping cream
- 4 eggs
- 1 cup pork rind
- Avocado oil, as needed for frying

Directions

1. Prepare the onion and for this, remove ¼ top off the onion, flip it cut-side-down and then cut it into quarters in such a way that there is only ¼-inch space from the onion nub. Cut the quarters into eights and then cut them into sixteenths.
2. Sprinkle coconut flour generously over the onion until each petal and the bottom of the onion have coated.
3. Prepare the egg wash and for this, take a medium bowl, crack the eggs in it, whisk in the cream until blended, and then spoon half of this mixture over the onion until each petal and the bottom of the onion have coated.
4. Take a separate medium bowl, place pork rind in it, add all the seasonings, stir until mixed, and then coat onion inside out with this mixture.
5. Repeat by pouring the remaining egg wash over the onion and dredge again into pork rind mixture.
6. Transfer onion onto a plate and then freeze it for 1 hour.
7. When ready to cook, take a large pot, place it over medium-high heat, fill it two-third with oil, and bring it to 300 degrees F temperature.
8. Then lower the frozen onion into the oil, petal-side-down, cook for 1 month, switch heat to medium-low level, flip the onion and fry it for 3 minutes.
9. Transfer onion to a plate lined with paper towels and let it rest for 5 minutes.
10. Serve the onion with dipping sauce.

Nutrition: 514 Calories 30.3g Fats 47.2g Proteins 10g Carbs

52. Pepperoni Chips

Preparation Time: 5'

Servings: 2

Cooking Time: 8'

Ingredients

- 30 pepperoni slices

Directions

1. Switch on the oven, set it to 400 degrees F, then set the baking rack in the middle and let it preheat. Meanwhile, take a sheet pan or two, line with parchment paper, and then spread pepperoni slices o with some spacing between each slice.
2. Bake the pepperoni slices for 4 minutes, then pat dry them with paper towels and then continue baking them for 4 minutes until nicely golden brown.
3. When done, drain the pepperoni slices on paper towels and then serve.

Nutrition: 150 Calories 14g Fats 5g Protein 1g Carbs

53. Mac 'n Cheese

Preparation Time: 20'

Servings: 12

Cooking Time: 20'

Ingredients

- 4 or 5 tablespoons flour
- ¼ teaspoon each of ground white pepper & Red-Hot Sauce
- 2 or 3 cups half and half
- ½ teaspoon Creole Seasoning or Essence
- 4 tablespoons butter, plus 2 tablespoons, plus 1 tablespoon
- 8 ½ ounces Parmigiano-Reggiano parmesan cheese, grated
- ¼ cup breadcrumbs, fresh
- 1-pound elbow macaroni
- ½ teaspoon garlic, minced
- 4 ounces each of cheddar cheese, gruyere cheese & Fontina cheese, grated
- ¾ teaspoon salt

Directions

1. Over low heat in a heavy, medium saucepan; heat 3 or 4 tablespoons of butter until melted. Add the flour; turn to combine & cook for 3 to 4 minutes, stirring constantly. Increase the heat to medium; slowly whisk in the half and half. Cook for 4 to 5 minutes, until thickened, stirring frequently. Remove from the heat and season with 4 ounces of the grated parmesan, hot sauce, pepper, and salt. Give the ingredients a good stir until cheese is completely melted & sauce is smooth. Cover & set aside.
2. Preheat your oven to 340 F in advance.
3. Fill a pot with water; bring it to a boil. Add the macaroni and salt to taste, stir well. Bring it to a boil again. Once done, decrease the heat to a low boil & continue to cook until macaroni is al dente, for 5 minutes. Drain the macaroni in a colander and put the macaroni in the pot. Add 2 tablespoons of butter and garlic; stir until everything blends. Add the bechamel sauce; stir until combined well. Set aside until ready to use.
4. Grease a 3-quart casserole or baking dish using the leftover butter & set aside. Combine the leftover parmesan cheese together with cheddar, fontina, and gruyere cheeses in a large bowl; toss until combined well.
5. Place 1/3 of the macaroni in the prepared baking dish. Add 1/3 of the mixed cheeses on top. Top with another third of the macaroni and another third of the mixture of cheese. Repeat with the leftover macaroni & cheese mixture. Combine the breadcrumbs together with leftover grated parmesan & the Essence in a small bowl; toss until combined well. Sprinkle this on top of the macaroni and cheese.
6. Bake until the macaroni & cheese is bubbly and hot, and the top is golden brown, for 40 to 45 minutes. Remove from oven & let sit for 5 minutes before serving.

Nutrition: 143 Calories 11g Fats 8g Protein 4g Carbs

54. Red Lobster Fudge Overboard

Preparation Time: 10'

Servings: 4

Cooking Time: 15'

Ingredients

For Pecan Brownies:
- 13 x 9 family size package of brownie mix
- Olive oil, required per the package Directions
- Egg (required as per the number mentioned on the package)
- ½ cup pecans, chopped

For Chocolate Sauce:
- ½ cup butter
- 4 unsweetened chocolate squares
- 1 can evaporated milk (12 ounces)
- 3 cups sugar
- ½ teaspoon salt
- For Whipped Cream:
- 1 can of canned whip whipped cream

Directions

For Pecan Brownies
1. Follow the Directions mentioned on the brownie mix and then add approximately ½ cup of the chopped pecans. Pour the prepared mixture into a large pan. Bake as per the Directions mentioned on the package.

For Chocolate Sauce:
2. Over low heat in a large, heavy saucepan; melt the butter & chocolate, stirring constantly. Slowly add the sugar, alternately with evaporated milk, starting & ending with sugar; continue to stir until smooth, for 5 minutes, over medium heat. Stir in the salt.

For Whipped Cream:
3. Microwave the chocolate sauce and brownie in separate dishes; ensure it's hot. After micro-waving the brownie, place a scoop of ice cream on top. Drizzle the hot chocolate sauce on top of the ice cream and then top with the whipped cream.

Nutrition: 169 Calories 10g Fat 19g Carbs 33g Protein

55. Chocolate Wave

Preparation Time: 25'	**Servings:** 6

Cooking Time: 5H 15'

Ingredients

- 4 organic eggs, large
- 1 cup sugar
- 2 ½ teaspoons cornstarch
- ¾ cup butter
- 4 egg yolks
- 1 cup semisweet chocolate chips
- 1 ½ teaspoon Grand Marnier

For White-Chocolate Truffle
- 3 tablespoons heavy cream
- 6 ounces white chocolate
- 2 tablespoons Grand Marnier
- 3 tablespoons softened butter

Directions

1. Over medium-low heat in a double boiler; melt the butter. Add in the chocolate chips; continue to heat until the mixture is completely melted.
2. Combine cornstarch and sugar in a large-sized mixing bowl. Add the chocolate mixture into the sugar mixture; beat well.
3. Combine four yolks with four eggs & Grand Marnier in a separate bowl. Add this to the chocolate mixture; continue to beat until mixed well. Cover & let chill for overnight.
4. For Truffle: Over low heat in a double boiler; melt the white chocolate with heavy cream. Add Grand Marnier and butter; give the ingredients a good stir until completely smooth. Chill for overnight.
5. Lightly coat 5-ounce ramekins with butter & then dust with flour, filling approximately 1/3 of the chilled chocolate mixture. Add a rounded tablespoon of the truffle mixture. Fill to the top with the chocolate mixture.
6. Bake for 15 minutes at 450 F. Let the cakes to sit for 15 to 20 minutes before inverting. Run a knife around the edges to loosen. Serve with raspberries, chocolate sauce, and/or ice cream.

Nutrition: 302 Calories 22g Fat 28g Carbs 35g Protein

56. Houston's Apple Walnut Cobbler

| Preparation Time: | 15' | Servings: | 6 |

| Cooking Time: | 30' |

Ingredients

- 3 large Granny Smith apples, peeled and diced
- 1½ cups walnuts, coarsely chopped
- 1 cup all-purpose flour
- 1 cup brown sugar
- 1 teaspoon cinnamon
- Pinch of nutmeg
- 1 large egg
- ½ cup (1 stick) butter, melted
- Vanilla ice cream
- Caramel sauce, for drizzling

Directions

1. Preheat oven to 350°F. Lightly grease an 8-inch square baking dish. Spread diced apple over the bottom of the baking dish.
2. Sprinkle with walnuts. In a bowl, mix together flour, sugar, cinnamon, nutmeg, and egg to make a coarse-textured mixture.
3. Sprinkle over the apple-walnut layer. Pour melted butter over the whole mixture. Bake until fragrant and crumb top is browned (about 30 minutes). Serve warm topped with scoops of vanilla ice cream.
4. Drizzle with caramel sauce.

Nutrition: 611 Calories 36g Fat 69g Carbs 8g Protein

57. Papa John's Cinnapie

Preparation Time: 5'

Servings: 12

Cooking Time: 12'

Ingredients

- 1 whole pizza dough
- 1 tablespoon melted butter
- 2 tablespoons cinnamon, or to taste

Topping
- ¾ cup flour
- ½ cup white sugar
- 1/3 cup brown sugar
- 2 tablespoons oil
- 2 tablespoons shortening

Icing
- 1½ cups powdered sugar
- 3 tablespoons milk
- ¾ teaspoon vanilla

Directions

1. Preheat oven to 460°F. Grease or spray a pizza pan or baking sheet.
2. Brush the dough evenly with melted butter. Sprinkle with cinnamon. Place the ingredients for the topping in a bowl and toss together with a fork.
3. Sprinkle topping over the dough. Bake until fragrant and lightly browned at the edges (about 10–12 minutes). Mix the icing ingredients together in a bowl. If too thick, gradually add in a little more milk. Drizzle icing over warm pizza

Nutrition: 560 Calories 90g Carbs 19g Fat 8g Protein

58. Olive Garden's Cheese Ziti Al Forno

Preparation Time:	10'

Servings:	8

Cooking Time:	35'

Ingredients

- 1 lb. Ziti
- 4 tbsp Butter
- 2 cloves Garlic
- 4 tbsp All-purpose flour
- 2 cups Half & Half
- A dash of Black pepper
- Kosher salt (as desired)
- 3 cups Marinara
- 1 cup - grated Parmesan - divided
- 2 cups Shredded mozzarella - divided

Other Shredded Cheese:
- ½ cup Fontina
- ½ cup Romano
- ½ cup Ricotta
- ½ cup Panko breadcrumbs

The garnish:
- Fresh Parsley

Directions

1. Warm the oven to reach 375° Fahrenheit.
2. Spritz the casserole dish with cooking oil spray. Prepare a large pot of boiling - salted water to cook the ziti until al dente. Drain and set it to the side.
3. Mince the garlic. Shred/grate the cheese and chop the parsley.
4. Make the alfredo. Heat the skillet using the medium temperature setting to melt the butter. Toss in the garlic to sauté for about half a minute. Whisk in flour and simmer until the sauce is bubbling (1-2 min.).
5. Whisk in the Half-and-Half and simmer. Stir in ½ cup parmesan, pepper, and salt. Cook it until the sauce thickens (2-3 min.). Stir in the marinara, one cup of mozzarella, Romano, fontina, and ricotta. Fold in the pasta. Dump it into the casserole dish.
6. Combine ½ cup of the parmesan and the breadcrumbs. Sprinkle it over the top of the dish. Set the timer and bake until browned as desired and bubbly (30 min.). Garnish with parsley and serve.

Nutrition: 272 Calories 20g Fat 25g Carbs 23g Protein

59. Chipotle's Refried Beans

Preparation Time: 5'

Servings: 6

Cooking Time: 5'

Ingredients

- 1-pound dried pinto beans
- 6 cups warm water
- ½ cup bacon fat
- 2 teaspoons salt
- 1 teaspoon cumin
- ½ teaspoon black pepper
- ½ teaspoon cayenne pepper

Directions

1. Rinse and drain the pinto beans. Check them over and remove any stones. Place the beans in a Dutch oven and add the water. Bring the pot to a boil, reduce the heat, and simmer for 2 hours, stirring frequently.
2. When the beans are tender, reserve ½ cup of the boiling water and drain the rest. Heat the bacon fat in a large, deep skillet. Add the beans 1 cup at a time, mashing and stirring as you go. Add the spices and some of the cooking liquid if the beans are too dry.

Nutrition: 100 Calories 18g Carbs 1g Fat 6g Protein

60. Low Fat Veggie Quesadilla

Preparation Time: 10'

Servings: 2

Cooking Time: 5'

Ingredients

- ½ tablespoon canola oil
- ½ cup mushrooms, chopped
- ½ cup carrot, grated
- 1/3 cup broccoli, sliced
- 2 tablespoons onion, finely chopped
- 1 tablespoon red bell pepper, finely chopped
- 1 teaspoon soy sauce
- 1 dash cayenne pepper
- 1 dash black pepper
- 1 dash salt
- 2 flour tortillas
- ¼ cup cheddar cheese, grated
- ¼ cup mozzarella cheese, grated
- ¼ cup sour cream
- ¼ cup salsa, medium or mild to taste
- ¼ cup shredded lettuce

Directions

1. Heat oil in a large skillet. Add mushrooms, carrots, broccoli, onion, and bell pepper. Stir-fry over medium-high heat for about 5 minutes. Pour in soy sauce, then season with cayenne, salt, and pepper. Transfer vegetables onto a plate. Set aside.
2. In the same skillet, heat first tortilla. Top with cheddar and mozzarella cheeses, followed by the cooked vegetables. Cover with the second tortilla. Cook for about 1 minute on each side or until cheeses are runny. Cut into slices. Serve hot with sour cream, salsa, and shredded lettuce on the side.

Nutrition: 186 Calories 12g Fat 18g Carbs 25g Protein

61. Garlic Mashed Potatoes

Preparation Time: 20'

Servings: 4

Cooking Time: 1 H

Ingredients

- 1 medium-sized bulb garlic, fresh
- 2 pounds red-skinned potatoes
- ½ cup milk
- ½ cup heavy cream
- ¼ cup butter
- Salt and pepper to taste

Directions

1. Preheat the oven to 400°F. Wrap whole garlic bulb with aluminum foil and bake it for 45 minutes, until the garlic softens. Remove it from the oven and let it cool in its wrapping.
2. Once cool, unwrap the garlic, peel off the outer layer, and squeeze the cooked pulp out. Set it aside. In the meantime, cut the potatoes and wash them, don't remove the skin and put them in a saucepan. Add water just to cover the potatoes. Boil until it cooks thoroughly for about 20 minutes.
3. Drain the water and add the other ingredients. Use the hands to mash. Lumps can be left, depending on your preference. Serve.

Nutrition: 254 Calories 16g Fat 24g Carbs 31g Protein

62. Vegetable Medley

Preparation Time: 15'

Servings: 4

Cooking Time: 10'

Ingredients

- ½ pound cold, fresh zucchini, sliced in half-moons
- ½ pound cold, fresh yellow squash, sliced in half-moons
- ¼ pound cold red pepper, julienned in strips ¼-inch thick
- ¼ pound cold carrots, cut into ¼-inch strips a few inches long
- ¼ pound cold red onions, thinly sliced
- 1 cold, small corn cob, cut crosswise in 1" segments
- 3 tablespoons cold butter or margarine
- 1 teaspoon salt
- 1 teaspoon sugar
- ½ teaspoon granulated garlic
- 1 teaspoon Worcestershire sauce
- 1 teaspoon soy sauce
- 2 teaspoons fresh or dried parsley

Directions

1. Wash, peel, and cut your vegetables as appropriate. In a saucepan, heat the butter over medium-high heat. Once it is hot, add salt, sugar, and garlic. Add the carrots, squash, and zucchini, and when they start to soften, add the rest of the vegetables and cook for a couple of minutes.
2. Add the Worcestershire sauce, soy sauce, and parsley. Stir to combine and coat the vegetables. When all the vegetables are cooked to your preference, serve.

Nutrition: 276 Calories 21g Fat 22g Carbs 30g Protein

63. Mega Mango Smoothie

Preparation Time: 10'

Servings: 4

Cooking Time: 1H 10'

Ingredients

- 1 can of brownie mix
- Ice cream, vanilla, to serve
- Hot Caramel sauce, to serve

Directions

1. Set the oven's temperature to exactly 350° F; cut the foil strips to line the giant muffin tin cups;
2. Lay the strips in crisscross-layer form for use as a handle for lifting when the brownies are made. Spray the foil in the kitchen spray pan; Prepare the brownie batter as indicated. Divide the batter between the muffin pans. The muffin cups can be about ¾ full;
3. Set the muffin pan on a heating sheet with the edges and start baking in the preheated oven for 40 to 50 minutes approximately; Remove the muffin pan from your oven and let it cool in the mold for 5 minutes approximately, then take to a rack to cool for another 10 minutes;
4. To loosen the sides of each brownie, you can use an icing spatula or a knife and then use the handles to lift the muffin pan. Serve a hot brownie on a plate with hot caramel sauce and a scoop of vanilla ice cream.

Nutrition: 206 Calories 24g Fat 24g Carbs 29g Protein

64. Lasagna with Feta and Black Olives

Preparation Time: 10'

Servings: 4

Cooking Time: 15'

Ingredients

- 8 lasagna sheets
- 600 gr of diced tomatoes
- Dried basil and oregano
- Salt and black pepper
- 1 sugar
- +/- 300 ml of béchamel
- 1 jar of pitted kalamata black olives
- +/- 150 gr of block feta
- A little grated cheese to brown
- A mixture of dried Greek herbs and Olive oil

Directions

1. Heat a touch olive oil in a saucepan or frying pan. Add the diced tomatoes, sugar, dried basil and oregano, salt and pepper (dose in step with your taste). Let simmer for at least 1/2 hour. Prepare your béchamel as you commonly do. Drain the olives and dice the feta.
2. Spread a little tomato and béchamel sauce within the bottom of a gratin dish, location 2 sheets of lasagna, tomato sauce, béchamel, black olives, and diced feta. Continue identically till all the ingredients are used up. Finish with béchamel, sprinkle with grated cheese, and sprinkle with Greek herbs.
3. Finally, bake at 180 ° C for 30 to 40 minutes and serve immediately.

Nutrition: 270 calories 16g total fats 11g protein

65. Easy Copycat Monterey's Little Mexico Queso

Preparation Time: 15'

Servings: 6

Cooking Time: 10'

Ingredients

- 1/2 cup of chopped yellow onion
- 1/2 cup of finely chopped celery
- 2 large green peppers such as Anaheim or Hatch, finely diced
- 2 tablespoons of butter
- 1 pound of American cheese
- 1/3 cup milk

Directions

1. The real mystery of flavored cheese is to fry vegetables till they're almost wholly cooked when you begin adding a little crunch in your American cheese.
2. Place the chopped onion, thinly sliced celery, and diced pepper in a casserole over medium warmness, upload tablespoons of oil, and cook until the onion is transparent. Put in a medium bowl, American cheese, sautéed onions, and milk. Heat until low or medium warmness melts the cheese.

Nutrition: 226 Calories 4g Carbohydrates 9g Protein 18g Fat

66. Fried Keto Cheese with Mushrooms

Preparation Time: 10'

Servings: 4

Cooking Time: 20'

Ingredients

- 300 g mushrooms
- 300 g halloumi cheese
- 75 g butter 10 green olives
- salt and ground black pepper
- 125 ml mayonnaise (optional)

Directions

1. Rinse and trim the mushrooms and chop or slice them. Heat the right quantity of butter in a pan in which they match and halloumi cheese and mushrooms.
2. Fry the mushrooms over medium heat for 3-5 minutes till golden brown. If vital, add extra butter and fry the halloumi cheese for a few minutes on every side. Stir the mushrooms occasionally.
3. Lower the warmness towards the end. Serve with olives.

Nutrition: 169 calories 17g total fats 10g protein

67. Mushroom Recipe Stuffed with Cheese, Spinach, and Bacon

| Preparation Time: | 10' | Servings: | 4 |

| Cooking Time: | 15' |

Ingredients

- 18 large mushrooms
- 4 strips of bacon cut into small cubes
- 2 butter spoons
- 2 tablespoons chopped onion
- ¾ cup grated fontina cheese
- 150 g spinach leaves chopped into large pieces
- Kosher Salt and freshly ground black pepper

Directions

1. Preheat the oven to 200 ° C. Cover a baking sheet with parchment paper. Wash the mushrooms. Remove the stems and locate the lids with the rounded sides down at the baking sheet. Chop the stems and reserve.
2. In a skillet over medium warmness, fry the bacon reduce into small cubes until crispy, drains. Leave approximately a tablespoon of bacon inside the pan. Add tablespoons of butter to the pan and add the chopped mushroom stems and chopped onion. Cook until the onion is translucent.
3. Add the spinach to the pan and cook until 3 minutes. Drain and transfer the aggregate to a bowl to cool. Add the bacon and half of a cup of cheese to the slightly cooled spinach aggregate. Stir to combine the components.
4. Try and upload Salt and freshly ground black pepper. Fill the mushrooms and cover each one with a touch extra fontina cheese. Bake for 15 minutes or until cheese melts and browns slightly.

Nutrition: 164 calories 18g total fats 12g protein

68. Shrimp Nachos with Avocado and Tomato Salsa

Preparation Time: 5'

Servings: 6

Cooking Time: 15'

Ingredients

Salsa
- 2 ripe Hass avocados, diced ¼ inch
- 1 large ripened tomato, free of stems and seeds, cut into ¼-inch dice
- 2 tablespoons fresh lime juice
- 1 tablespoon finely chopped fresh coriander leaves
- 1 garlic clove, minced or garlic press
- ½ teaspoon ground cumin
- Kosher Salt
- Freshly ground black pepper
- 1 ear of sweet corn, peeled
- Extra virgin olive oil
- ½ teaspoon ground cumin
- ¼ teaspoons chipotle chili powder
- 20 jumbo shrimps (count of 21/30), shelled and deveined, without the tail
- 170 grams tortilla chips
- 225 grams of coarsely grated sharp cheddar cheese
- 4 green onions (white and pale green parts only), thinly sliced, green and white parts separated
- 1 small jalapeño pepper, seeded, finely chopped
- 1 tablespoon chopped fresh coriander

Directions

1. Combine the components for the salsa sauce. Season with ½ tsp. Salt and ¼ tsp. Of pepper.
2. Set the grill at 350 to 450 degrees and preheat the perforated grill for 10 mins.
3. Lightly brush the corn with oil, then grill directly on the cooking grids over medium warmth, with the lid closed and turning it if necessary, till it is browned in places and tender, eight to 12 mins. Leave to cool, then cut the grains from the cob.
4. Mix the cumin, the chili powder, ½ tsp. Salt and ¼ tsp. Of pepper. Brush the shrimp with oil, then sprinkle the spice aggregate lightly. Divide the shrimp in a single layer on the baking sheet and grill over medium direct heat, with the lid closed and turning once till they're firm to the touch and opaque inside the center, 2 to 4 minutes. With protecting barbeque gloves, do away with the baking sheet and the shrimp from the warmth and transfer the shrimp to a piece surface. Cut every shrimp in 1/2 crosswise, crosswise. Prepare the grill for oblique cooking over medium warmness (350 to 450 ° F).
5. Spread the tortilla at the bottom of a 12-inch solid iron skillet. Scatter cheese calmly over potato chips, then corn, the white part of green onions, and jalapeño pepper. Cook over indirect medium warmth, with the barbecue lid, closed, for 8 to 10 minutes, till the cheese has melted. During the final 2 mins of cooking, upload the shrimp on the nachos. Remove from warmth and garnish with the inexperienced a part of the green onions and the coriander. Serve warm with salsa.

Nutrition: 204 calories 18.1g total fats 12g protein

69. Mimosa Eggs with Truffle

Preparation Time: 5'

Servings: 6

Cooking Time: 15'

Ingredients

- 6 Eggs
- 1/2 cup Mayonnaise
- 2 c. tablespoons Chives finely chopped
- 1-2 tsp. tablespoon truffle oil of excellent quality
- 2-3 slices crispy bacon, crumbled
- Salt and pepper
- Pastry bag or Ziploc bag

Directions

1. Boil the eggs for approximately 8 minutes. Let cool and peel the shell. Cut in 1/2 lengthwise, cast off the yolk with a small spoon, and place in a bowl with mayonnaise, truffle oil, salt, pepper, and half of the chives. Mash the mixture with a fork or use a small blender. Put all the mixtures in a piping bag or a Ziploc bag. Arrange the egg whites on a pleasing plate and fill them with the combination. Garnish with the rest of the chives and bacon. You can end with a little fleur de sel and a touch extra truffle oil, if necessary.

Nutrition: 125 Calories 18g total fats 10.9g protein

70. Shrimp Tempura

Preparation Time: 10'

Servings: 6

Cooking Time: 5'

Ingredients

- 1/2 kg clean shrimp
- Garlic and salt to season shrimp
- 4 whole eggs
- 5 tablespoons of flour
- 1 Red Seasonal Envelope or Seasonal for Fish Oil for frying

Directions

1. Season the smooth shrimp with garlic and salt and set aside. Beat whole eggs till soft, upload a pinch of Salt, the seasoning and flour, and beat appropriately with a fork until smooth.
2. Gradually dip the shrimp on this batter and fry in warm oil. When browning the dough, take away with a slotted spoon and drain on an absorbent paper towel. Serve warm as it tastes or maybe with white rice and shrimp sauce.

Nutrition: 170 calories 14g total fats 10g protein

71. Copycat Chili's Southwest Egg Rolls

| Preparation Time: | 5' | Servings: | 4 |

| Cooking Time: | 15' |

Ingredients

- 8 oz chicken breast
- 1 teaspoon of olive oil vegetable oil is fine
- 1 tablespoon of olive oil vegetable oil is fine
- 1/4 cup chopped red bell pepper
- 1/4 cup chopped spring onions
- 1/2 cup frozen corn
- 1/2 cup canned black beans
- 1/4 cup frozen spinach
- 2 tsp of pickled jalapeno pepper
- 1 teaspoon of taco spice
- 3/4 cup of grated Monterey Jack cheese
- 8/7-inch flour tortillas
- 1/4 cup mashed fresh avocados (about half an avocado)
- 1 pack of Ranch Dressing Mix
- 1/2 cup milk
- 1/2 cup mayonnaise
- 2 tablespoons of chopped tomatoes
- 1 tablespoon of chopped onions

Directions

1. Season with salt and black pepper to the fowl. Brush the fowl breast with olive oil. Grill on a grill with medium heat. Cook on each side for five to 7 mins. Cut the hen into tiny pieces. Set apart the fowl.
2. Sauté till tender red pepper. Refer to the aggregate of the green onion, rice, black beans, spinach, and pickled jalapenos. Attach the seasoning of taco. Via the sun.
3. Place the tortillas in the same quantities of the filing, identical amounts of chicken, and pinnacle with cheese. Fold and roll-up on the ends of the tortilla. Make positive the tortillas are very tight to roll. To defend the pin with toothpicks.
4. We are growing enough vegetable oil in a big pot to cover the pan's backside through 4 inches. Heat up to 350°C. Deep fry the rolls of the eggs until golden brown. It ought to take seven to eight mins. When extracting golden from oil, growing it on a rack of wire.
5. Prepare a container of mayonnaise half-cup ranch dressing mix and buttermilk half of cup. Remove the aggregate 1/4 cup of mashed avocado. In a blender, pump the combination till the sauce is mixed.

Nutrition: 502 Calories 42g Carbohydrates 19g Protein 28g Fat

72. Ham and Cheese Grinders

Preparation Time: 10'

Servings: 2

Cooking Time: 5'

Ingredients

- 300 g of refrigerated pizza dough
- 2 cloves of garlic
- 2 tablespoons olive oil
- 1 teaspoon Italian seasoning
- ¼ cup grated Parmesan cheese
- 1 cup shredded mozzarella cheese
- 250 g sliced ham
- 1 egg
- Chopped fresh parsley
- Marinara sauce

Directions

1. Gather all the elements to make ham and cheese grinders.
2. Preheat the oven to 180 ° C. Add the chopped garlic and the Italian seasoning to the olive oil.
3. Spread the chilled pizza dough in a large rectangle and reduce the choppy edges if desired.
4. Distribute the olive oil combination over the dough and sprinkle the grated Parmesan cheese and 1/2 of the grated mozzarella cheese over the dough floor.
5. Cowl the surface of the cheese with cooked ham and sprinkle the surface with the rest of the grated mozzarella cheese. Roll the dough as you could see inside the image.
6. Seal the edges of the dough through becoming a member of the dough and cut into nine parts. Place the ham and cheese grinders on a baking sheet lined with parchment paper.
7. Beat the egg with a teaspoon of warm water until well mixed. Brush the egg on the top and sides of the grinders.
8. Bake the grinders for 15 to twenty minutes or till they're fluffy and golden brown.
9. Cover the grinders with chopped fresh parsley and serve right away with marinara sauce.

Nutrition: 190 calories 17g total fats 11g protein

73. Mozzarella Cheese Sticks Recipe

Preparation Time: 5'

Servings: 10

Cooking Time: 5'

Ingredients

- ¼ cup flour
- 1 cup breadcrumbs
- 2 eggs
- 1 tablespoon milk
- 500 g mozzarella cheese
- 1 cup of vegetable oil
- 1 cup marinara sauce

Directions

1. Gather all the elements of mozzarella cheese sticks then mix eggs and milk together in a medium bowl. Cut the mozzarella into sticks 2 x 2 cm thick.
2. Cover each mozzarella cane with flour. Then dip them inside the egg and then within the breadcrumbs.
3. Dip the mozzarella sticks lower back into the egg and skip them in breadcrumbs.
4. Take to the freezer earlier than frying. Heat the oil within the pan and prepare dinner the mozzarella cheese sticks for approximately a minute on every aspect or until well browned.
5. Drain the cheese sticks on paper napkins and serve with marinara sauce or pizza sauce.

Nutrition: 168 calories 19g total fats 12g protein

74. Copycat Mac and Cheese with Smoked Gouda Cheese and Pumpkin

Preparation Time: 5'

Servings: 2

Cooking Time: 15'

Ingredients

- 1 1/2 tbsp olive oil
- 120 grams of fresh baguette torn into small pieces
- 2 teaspoons fresh thyme leaves
- 1/4 cup grated Parmesan
- 450 grams of spiral pasta (or penne)
- 4 tablespoons salted butter
- 4 tablespoons of flour
- 3 cups room temp milk
- 1 cup canned pumpkin puree
- 2 cups smoked and chopped gouda cheese
- 2 cups cut sharp cheddar
- Kosher Salt

Directions

1. Preheat oven to 190ºC. Grease a large pan with nonstick cooking spray.
2. In a massive bowl, combine the cornbread, olive oil, thyme, and ½ tsp kosher Salt. Put in greased pan and bake till golden brown (12 to 15 minutes). Remove from oven, incorporate grated Parmesan, and set aside.
3. In a large pan of boiling salted water, cook the pasta al dente in line with package deal Directions. Drain the water and set aside the pasta.
4. Melt butter in a pan over medium heat. Incorporate the flour and cook dinner, continually stirring, till the aggregate starts to thicken (about one to mins).
5. Gradually include the milk, continually mixing until it paperwork a lightly thickened sauce (five to six minutes). Add the mashed pumpkin and two teaspoons of kosher salt. Beat till included adequately into the sauce. Lower the warmth and location, the gouda and cheddar cheeses, mixing nicely until melted.
6. Incorporate the cooked pasta into the sauce. Transfer the whole lot to a prepared baking sheet. Sprinkle with toasted breadcrumbs. Put in oven and let till golden and blistered (about 20 mins). Serve immediately.

Nutrition: 159 calories 15g total fats 12g protein

75. Baked Buffalo Meatballs

Preparation Time: 5'

Servings: 4

Cooking Time: 20'

Ingredients

- 350 gram of ground chicken meat
- 1 clove of minced garlic
- 1/4 cup of ground bread
- 2 tablespoons grated parmesan
- 2 teaspoons fresh celery leaves
- 1 egg
- 1/4 cup flour
- salt and pepper to taste
- 1/2 cup botanica sauce (Valentina or buffalo botanica)
- 2 tablespoons melted butter
- 1 tablespoon apple cider vinegar
- garlic powder and celery salt to taste for blue cheese dressing
- 1/3 cup of mayonnaise
- 1/3 cup sour cream
- 1 tablespoon lemon juice
- 1/4 cup blue cheese salt and pepper to taste

Directions

1. Preheat the oven to 190°C Mix the chook with the garlic, the ground bread, the Parmesan, the celery, the egg, and the flour. Form balls together with your arms and region them on a tray with foil; bake for 18 mins.
2. Mix the botanica sauce with the melted butter and season with garlic powder and celery salt, bathe on this sauce every meatball as quickly as they go away the oven.
3. To make the dressing, blend the cream, mayonnaise, lemon, and half of the blue cheese; upload the relaxation of the crumbled cheese and season to taste. Serve the meatballs with chopsticks observed via blue cheese dressing.

Nutrition: 170 calories 16g total fats 13g protein

Chapter 3

Old and Modern Fruit Salad Recipes

76. Apple Pomegranate Salad: Wendy's™ Copycat

Preparation Time: 25'

Servings: 8

Cooking Time: 0'

Ingredients

- 1 bunch/8 cups romaine
- ½ cup Pomegranate seeds
- ½ cup Toasted and chopped walnuts/pecans
- ½ cup Shredded parmesan cheese
- 1 Granny Smith apple
- 1 tbsp Lemon juice
- ¼ cup Olive oil
- ¼ cup White wine vinegar
- 2 tbsp Sugar
- ¼ tsp Salt

Directions

1. Tear the romaine into pieces and combine with the pecans, pomegranate seeds, and cheese in a salad bowl. Chop and toss in the apple with lemon juice. Whisk the rest of the fixings until blended in a small mixing container. Toss it together and serve.

Nutrition: 300 calories 17.8g fats 2.4g protein

77. Cranberry Fruit Salad: The Famous Luby's Cafeteria™ Copycat

Preparation Time: 20'

Cooking Time: 0'

Servings: 8-10

Ingredients

- 1 Apple
- 12 oz Fresh cranberries
- 1 Banana
- 1 Orange
- 1 cup Broken walnuts/pecans

Directions

1. Peel the banana. Rinse and sort the cranberries and peel the orange removing the pith.
2. Whisk the sugar and water in a saucepan until the crystals are dissolved. Dump the cranberries into the pan and lower the heat once it's boiling. Simmer until most of the cranberries have popped or for four to five minutes, stirring occasionally.
3. Transfer the pan of cranberries from the burner and set the pan to the side to cool for a few minutes. Quarter the apple, core, and chop, adding it to the cooled cranberries.
4. Chop the banana and orange, adding it to cranberries with the nuts. Mix and pop it into the fridge until time to eat (at least four hours or - even better - overnight).

Nutrition: 289 calories 16g fats 4g protein

78. Fuji Apple Chicken Salad: Panera Bread™ Copycat

Preparation Time: 15'

Servings: 4

Cooking Time: 10'

Ingredients

- 10 oz mix of spring mix salad and chopped romaine
- ½ Red onion
- 2-3 Vine-ripened tomatoes
- 2 Chicken breasts
- 2 cups Apple chips
- ¾ cup Roasted pecan halves
- ½ cup Crumbled Gorgonzola cheese
- ¾ cup Vinaigrette - Panera™ Bread Fuji Apple

Directions

1. Do the prep. Thinly slice the onion and chop the salad. Shred the chicken. Combine each of the fixings in a large salad dish. Evenly distribute the salad and serve!

Nutrition: 250 calories 16g fats 3g protein

79. Market Salad: Chick-Fil-A™ Copycat

Preparation Time: 10'

Servings: 1-2

Cooking Time: 10'

Ingredients

- 1 cup Chicken breast
- 1 head Romaine lettuce
- 8 oz Baby greens
- ½ cup Red cabbage
- ½ cup Carrots
- Optional: Crumbled goat/blue cheese
- 1 Red apple
- 1 Green apple
- 1-pint Strawberries
- ¼ cup Blueberries

Directions

1. Do the prep. Cook and cool the chicken. Then chop/shred it. Tear the lettuce apart. Shred the carrots and cabbage. Cut the apples into chunks, and quarter the strawberries.
2. Combine each of the fixings in a salad bowl and serve with the vinaigrette.

Nutrition: 270 calories 15g fats 4g protein

80. Strawberry Poppyseed Salad: Panera™ Copycat

Preparation Time: 30'

Servings: 10

Cooking Time: 0'

Ingredients

- ¼ cup Sugar
- 1/3 cup Slivered almonds
- 8 cups Torn romaine lettuce
- 1 small Halved - thinly sliced onions
- 2 cups Halved fresh strawberries

The Dressing:
- 2 tbsp Sugar
- ¼ cup Mayo
- 1 tbsp Sour cream
- 1 tbsp 2% milk
- 2 ¼ tsp Cider vinegar
- 1 ½ tsp Poppy seeds

Directions

1. Pour the sugar into a small heavy skillet. Cook it and stir using the med-low temperature setting until melted and caramel-colored or for about ten minutes. Stir in the almonds until coated. Smear the mixture onto a layer of foil to cool.
2. Toss the romaine, onion, and strawberries in a large salad serving container. Combine the dressing fixings and toss them with the salad. Break the candied almonds into pieces and sprinkle over salad. Serve immediately.

Nutrition: 249 calories 16.9g fats 3.1g protein

81. Sweet Carrot Salad: Chick-Fil-A™ Copycat

Preparation Time: 35'

Cooking Time: 0'

Servings: 8

Ingredients

- 1 lb. Grated carrots
- 1 cup Crushed pineapple
- ½ cup Raisins
- 1 tbsp Honey
- 2 tbsp Mayonnaise
- 1 dash Lemon juice

Directions

1. Grate the carrots and mix in with the raisins, pineapple, and the rest of the fixings until evenly coated. Pop into the fridge to chill for about half an hour to meld the flavors before serving.

Nutrition: 239 calories 16.4g fats 12g protein

82. Waldorf Salad: Texas Luby's Cafeteria™ Copycat

| Preparation Time: | 15' + 2H - Chilling Time | Servings: | 8 |

| Cooking Time: | 0' |

Ingredients

- 4 cups Granny Smith apples
- 2 cups Canned pineapple tidbits
- 1 cup Celery
- ½ cup Mayonnaise
- ¼ cup Whipping cream
- 1 drop Vanilla extract
- 1 tbsp Powdered sugar
- 1 tbsp Chopped walnuts or pecans

Directions

1. Drain the pineapple, chop the celery, and cube the apples. Combine the pineapple, apples, celery, and mayo in a large mixing container, tossing gently.
2. In another mixing container, whip the cream using the high-speed setting with an electric mixer to create stiff peaks. Blend in the vanilla, sugar, and fruit. Cover in plastic and chill for a minimum of two hours. When it's time to serve, sprinkle with the nuts.

Nutrition: 259 calories 17.3g fats 5g protein

83. Cottage Cheese and Poppy Seed Mousse with Cherry Water

Preparation Time: 90'

Servings: 6

Cooking Time: 0'

Ingredients

- 50 g ground poppy seeds
- 6 tbsp Cherry water (at will)
- 5 sheets white gelatin
- 1 pack vanilla sugar
- 150 g sugar
- freshly squeezed juice of 1 lemon
- 250 g cream
- 500 g low-fat quark

Directions

1. Roast the poppy seeds in a non-fat pan over medium-high heat, stirring, until they smell. Deglaze with 60 ml water and possibly 3 tbsp cherry water, let the liquid boil down completely. Let the poppy seeds cool.
2. In the meantime, soak the gelatin in water according to the package. Mix the vanilla sugar, sugar, lemon juice, any remaining cherry water, and 50 g of cream until the sugar has dissolved. Add the curd and poppy seeds and stir until smooth. Whip the rest of the cream until stiff.
3. Squeeze out the gelatin and dissolve in a small saucepan over low heat. Add 1 tablespoon of curd cream, stir well, add a spoon and stir well again, then stir the gelatin quickly with a whisk under the remaining curd, fold in the cream. Cover the mousse and let it set in the fridge in about 5 hours.
4. Cut off the mousse with a tablespoon of cams and serve - for example, with spiced cherries or cassis pears.

Nutrition: 280 calories 16g fats 3g protein

84. Good Mood Fruit Salad

Preparation Time: 30'

Servings: 4

Cooking Time: 0'

Ingredients

- 1 Apple
- 150 g grapes
- 1 kiwi
- 1 banana
- 1 orange
- 2 tbsp dried cranberries (dried fruit shelf)
- 2 tbsp Agave syrup

Directions

1. Wash the apple and grapes. Peel the kiwi, banana, and orange. Cut everything into small pieces. (Bananas stay firmer if you quarter them lengthways and then cut them into thumb-thick slices - that makes cubes.) Mix the fruit and cranberries with the agave syrup.

Nutrition: 145 calories 14g fats 5g protein

85. Fruit Salad with Lemon Foam

Preparation Time: 30'

Servings: 4

Cooking Time: 0'

Ingredients

- 4th ripe nectarines
- 200 g Raspberries
- 1 tbsp Pistachio nuts
- 4th very fresh egg yolk (size M)
- 4 tbsp sugar
- Juice of 1 lemon
- 1/8 l prosecco (or non-alcoholic sparkling wine)

Directions

1. Peel the nectarines with a small sharp knife and cut the pulp into slices from the stone. Read out the raspberries, wash them carefully, and drain them on kitchen paper. Spread the fruit mixed in four glasses or on dessert plates. Roughly chop the pistachios.
2. Prepare a saucepan with a suitable metal mixing bowl for a hot water bath, pour approx. 5 cm of water into the saucepan and heat. Mix the egg yolks in the bowl with the sugar and whisk for 3-4 minutes with the whisk of the hand mixer.
3. Place the bowl over the hot water bath and pour the lemon juice and prosecco into the egg yolk cream while stirring continuously until an airy foam form. Pull out the bowl from the water bath and continue to beat the foam for 1-2 minutes until it is only lukewarm.
4. Pour the lemon foam over the fruit salads and sprinkle the pistachios. Serve the dessert immediately.

Nutrition: 225 calories 17.1g fats 4g protein

86. Vegan Amaranth Pudding with Fruit Salad

Preparation Time: 60'

Servings: 4

Cooking Time: 0'

Ingredients

- 200 g Amaranth grains
- 1 l soy milk
- 6 Apricots
- 2 tbsp Walnut kernels
- 4 tbsp Pomegranate seeds
- 60 g sugar
- Cinnamon powder
- 3 tbsp food starch
- 2 pack Bourbon vanilla sugar
- 1 pinch salt
- 300 g cold soy cream
- 1 pack Cream fixer

Directions

1. For the pudding on the evening before, cover the amaranth with sufficient water and let it swell for 12 hours. Pour into a colander the next day and drain. Boil the amaranth and soy milk in a saucepan, then cover and simmer over low heat for 25 minutes.
2. In the meantime, wash, halve, stone and cut the apricots for the fruit salad and cut them into wedges. Roughly chop the walnut kernels. Mix the apricot slices, nuts, pomegranate seeds, and 1 tablespoon of sugar, season with a pinch of cinnamon.
3. Mix the starch, vanilla sugar, remaining sugar, salt, and ½ tsp cinnamon. Stir the mix into the amaranth and let simmer for about 2 minutes. Let the pudding mixture cool lukewarm in the pot.
4. Whisk the soy cream with the hand mixer until foamy. Sprinkle in the cream fixer and continue beating until the cream is firm and foamy. Fold the whipped cream under the pudding mixture. Fill the pudding in four glasses and arrange the fruit salad on it.

Nutrition: 248 calories 14g fats 6g protein

87. Quick Fruit Salad with Sabayon

Preparation Time: 30'

Servings: 4

Cooking Time: 0'

Ingredients

- 2nd fully ripe figs
- 1 kiwi
- 100 g each seedless blue and green grape
- 100 g Strawberries
- 1 pear
- 6 tbsp freshly squeezed lime juice
- 2nd Egg yolks
- 1 tbsp sugar
- grated peel of 1 organic lime
- 1 tbsp chopped almonds

Directions

1. Wash the figs and quarter them lengthways. Peel the kiwi, quarter lengthways and slice transversely. Wash the grapes, pluck from the stems and cut in half.
2. Briefly rinse, clean, and halve the strawberries. Quarter the pear, core, peel, and cut into fine slices. Arrange the fruit decoratively on four plates, drizzle with 2 tablespoons of lime juice.
3. Mix the egg yolks with the sugar, 2 tablespoons of warm water, and the remaining lime juice and the grated lime peel in the kettle and beat in a hot, non-boiling water bath until the mixture is thick and creamy.
4. Remove from the water bath, continue to beat for 1-2 minutes next to the stove and spread lukewarm over the fruit. Sprinkle with the almonds.

Nutrition: 135 calories 14g fats 5g protein

88. Tropical Fruit Salad with Coconut Cream

Preparation Time: 60'

Servings: 4

Cooking Time: 0'

Ingredients

- 150 g small strawberries
- 100 g Raspberries
- 1 pear
- 1 Apple
- 1 banana
- 2nd Kiwi fruit
- 1 1/2 tbsp lemon juice
- 2 tbsp sugar
- 4 tbsp Grated coconut
- 150 g cream

Directions

1. Wash the strawberries carefully and cut out the sepals. Pick raspberries. Peel the pear, apple, banana, and kiwi fruit. Quarter the pear and apple, core, and cut into wedges. Slice the banana. Quarter the kiwis lengthways, separate the stalk from the center and cut the kiwis into thin slices.
2. Mix the lemon juice with 1 tablespoon of sugar, mix in the fruit and let marinate for 15-30 minutes.
3. Mix the grated coconut with 1 teaspoon of sugar in a pan and roast without fat while stirring over medium heat until golden yellow. Be careful not to burn them! Put on a plate.
4. Do not whip the cream until stiff, pour in the remaining sugar, and mix in the coconut flakes. Spread the fruit salad on plates and garnish with the coconut cream.

Nutrition: 295 Calories 14g fats 3.1g protein

89. Exotic Fruit Salad with Coconut-Lime Yoghurt

Preparation Time: 30'

Servings: 4

Cooking Time: 0'

Ingredients

- 3rd Tangerines
- 1 papaya
- 300 g Pineapple pulp
- 50 ml orange juice
- 5 tbsp Lime juice
- honey
- 300 g Greek or Turkish yogurt (10% fat)
- 50 g coconut cream

Directions

1. Peel the tangerines, divide them into individual segments, and divide them crosswise. Peel and halve the papaya, remove the seeds and dice the pulp. Dice the pineapple pulp as well.
2. Mix all the prepared fruits, add the orange juice, and 1 tablespoon of lime juice, and season with a little honey.
3. Place the yogurt with coconut cream and 4 tablespoons of lime juice in a blender jar and puree until smooth. Season the cream with honey to taste. Divide the coconut-lime yogurt into four deep plates and arrange the fruit on it.

Nutrition: 175 calories 16g fats 4.3g protein

90. Ginger Fruit Salad with Vanilla Sauce

Preparation Time: 60-90'

Servings: 6

Cooking Time: 0'

Ingredients

- 1 Vanilla bean
- 1/4 l milk
- 250 g cream
- 1 tbsp food starch
- 2nd fresh egg yolk
- 60 g sugar
- 1 ripe mango
- 3rd ripe peaches
- 1 small ripe honeydew melon
- 250 g Strawberries
- 1-piece fresh ginger (approx. 4 cm)
- 4th Stems of mint
- 1 Organic lime
- 70 g powdered sugar

Directions

1. Slice the vanilla pod for the sauce, scrape out the pulp. Put both in a saucepan with 200 ml milk and the cream and simmer for 5 minutes, stirring occasionally, over low heat.
2. In the meantime, mix the starch well with the egg yolks, remaining milk, and sugar. Pour into the pot while stirring and bring to the boil once, stirring constantly. Take it from the stove and let it cool off. (Fish out the pod before serving!)
3. For the salad, peel the mango thinly, cut diagonally from the core, and dice finely. Wash, halve, core, and dice peaches. Cut the melon into wedges, remove the seeds with a spoon, cut the pulp from the skin, and dice. Wash and clean the strawberries and quarter or halve them depending on their size.
4. Peel and finely chop the ginger. Wash the mint, pluck the leaves, and cut them into strips.
5. Wash the lime hot. Rub the peel finely, squeeze out the juice and mix both with sugar, ginger, and mint. Mix gently under the fruit and cover and let the salad cover in the refrigerator for 25-30 minutes.

Nutrition: 280 calories 14.1g fats 2.6g protein

91. Fruit Salad with Vanilla Sauce

Preparation Time: 30'

Servings: 10

Cooking Time: 0'

Ingredients

- 400 g Cream pudding with vanilla flavor
- 400 ml milk
- 1 kg fresh fruit (e.g., orange, banana, apple, berries, kiwi, grapes)

Directions

1. For the sauce, simply stir the cream pudding into the cold milk.
2. Wash and clean the fresh fruit. Halve or quarter larger fruits. Mix the fruit and eat with the sauce.

Nutrition: 135 calories 15.1g fats 5.1g protein

92. Fruit Salad with Yoghurt Cream

Preparation Time: 30'

Servings: 4

Cooking Time: 0'

Ingredients

- 1 Charentais melon
- 500 g soft seasonal fruit
- 50 g Pine nuts
- 2 tbsp Coconut flakes
- 1 cup Cream (200 ml)
- 1 parcel vanilla sugar
- 1 cup Vanilla Yogurt (150 g)

Directions

1. Divide the melon once, remove the seeds and scrape out the pulp with an ice cream spoon so that the peel is not destroyed. Cut the pulp into 1 cm cubes.
2. Wash the rest of the fruit well and cut it into small pieces. Mix all the fruit well in a large bowl and arrange it in the melon bowls. What no longer fits in the small bowls.
3. Roast the pine nuts briefly in a non-fat pan, add coconut flakes for a few seconds. Spread both evenly over the fruit salad.
4. For the yogurt cream, whip the cream stiffly together with the vanilla sugar using the hand mixer. Stir in the vanilla yogurt and let it flow in slowly just before the cream becomes really stiff. Serve with fruit salad.

Nutrition: 405 calories 14.9g fats 5.1g protein

Chapter 4

Old and Modern Dessert Recipes

93. Maple Butter Blondie

Preparation Time: 15'

Servings: 9

Cooking Time: 35'

Ingredients

- 1/3 cup butter, melted
- 1 cup brown sugar, packed
- 1 large egg, beaten
- 1 tablespoon vanilla extract
- ½ teaspoon baking powder
- 1/8 teaspoon baking soda
- 1/8 teaspoon salt
- 1 cup flour
- 2/3 cup white chocolate chips
- 1/3 cup pecans, chopped (or walnuts)
- Maple butter sauce
- ¾ cup maple syrup
- ½ cup butter
- ¾ cup brown sugar
- 8 ounces cream cheese, softened to room temp
- ¼ cup pecans, chopped
- Vanilla ice cream, for serving

Directions

1. Preheat the oven to 350°F and coat a 9x9 baking pan with cooking spray.
2. In a mixing bowl, combine the butter, brown sugar, egg, and vanilla, and beat until smooth. Sift in the baking powder, baking soda, salt, and flour, and stir until it is well incorporated. Fold in the white chocolate chips.
3. Bake for 20–25 minutes. While those are in the oven, prepare the maple butter sauce by combining the maple syrup and butter in a medium saucepan.
4. Cook over low heat until the butter is melted. Add the brown sugar and cream cheese. Stir constantly until the cream cheese has completely melted, then remove the pot from the heat. Remove the blondies from the oven and cut them into squares.
5. Top with vanilla ice cream, maple butter sauce, and chopped nuts.

Nutrition: 40g carbs 14g fats 3g protein

94. Apple Chimi Cheesecake

Preparation Time: 10'

Servings: 2

Cooking Time: 10'

Ingredients

- 2 (9 inches) flour tortillas
- ¼ cup granulated sugar
- ½ teaspoon cinnamon
- 3 ounces cream cheese, softened
- ½ teaspoon vanilla extract
- 1/3 cup apple, peeled and finely chopped
- Oil for frying
- Vanilla ice cream (optional)
- Caramel topping (optional)

Directions

1. Make sure your tortillas and cream cheese are at room temperature; this will make them both easier to work with. In a small bowl, combine the sugar and cinnamon.
2. In another mixing bowl, combine the cream cheese and vanilla until smooth. Fold in the apple. Divide the apple and cheese mixture in two and place half in the center of each tortilla. Leave at least an inch margin around the outside.
3. Fold the tortilla top to the middle, then the bottom to the middle, and then roll it up from the sides. Heat about half an inch of oil in a skillet over medium heat.
4. Place the filled tortillas into the skillet and fry on each side until they are golden brown. Transfer them to a plate lined with paper towels to drain any excess oil, then immediately coat them with the cinnamon and sugar. Serve with a scoop of ice cream.

Nutrition: 43g carbs 12g fats 5g protein

95. Triple Chocolate Meltdown

Preparation Time: 1H

Cooking Time: 30'

Servings: 8

Ingredients

- 2 cups heavy cream, divided
- 1 cup white chocolate chips
- 1 cup semi-sweet chocolate chips
- 1-pound bittersweet chocolate, chopped
- ½ cup butter, softened
- 6 eggs
- 1 ½ cups of sugar
- 1 ½ cups all-purpose flour
- Ice cream, for serving

Directions

1. Preheat the oven to 400°F.
2. Prepare 8 ramekins by first coating the inside with butter and then sprinkling them with flour so the bottom and sides are covered. Place them on a baking tray.
3. In a saucepan, bring 1 cup of heavy cream to a simmer. Remove it from the heat and add the white chocolate chips, stirring until the chocolate is melted and the mixture is smooth. Allow it to cool for about half an hour, stirring occasionally.
4. Repeat with the other cup of cream and the semi-sweet chocolate chips. In a double boiler, combine the bittersweet chocolate with the softened butter and stir until the chocolate is melted and the mixture is smooth. Remove the bowl from the heat and allow it to cool for about 10 minutes.
5. In a mixing bowl, beat the eggs and the sugar together for about 2 minutes, or until the mixture is foamy. Use a rubber spatula to fold in the bittersweet chocolate mixture. Turn the mixer to low and beat in the flour half a cup at a time, being careful not to overmix the batter.
6. Pour the batter evenly into the prepared ramekins and place the baking tray in the oven. Bake for about 18 minutes. When done, the cakes should have a slight crust but still be soft in the middle. Remove them from the oven when they have reached this look. If you cook them too long, you won't get the lava cake effect.
7. Let the ramekins sit on the tray for 2–3 minutes and then invert them onto serving plates. Drizzle some of both the semi-sweet and white chocolate sauces over the top and serve with a scoop of ice cream.

Nutrition: 39g carbs 15g fats 6g protein

96. Chocolate Mousse Dessert Shooter

Preparation Time: 30'

Servings: 4

Cooking Time: 0'

Ingredients

- 2 tablespoons butter
- 6 ounces semi-sweet chocolate chips (1 cup), divided
- 1 teaspoon vanilla
- 2 eggs, separated, at room temperature
- 2 tablespoons sugar
- ½ cup heavy cream
- 8 Oreo® cookies
- ½ cup prepared fudge sauce
- Canned whipped cream

Directions

1. Melt the butter and all but 1 tablespoon of the chocolate chips in a double boiler. When they are melted, stir in the vanilla and remove from the heat. Whisk in the egg yolks.
2. Beat the egg whites until they form soft peaks, and then fold them into the chocolate mixture. Beat the sugar and heavy cream in a separate bowl until it forms stiff peaks or is the consistency that you desire. Fold this into the chocolate mixture.
3. Crush the remaining chocolate chips into small pieces and stir them into the chocolate. Crush the Oreos. (You can either scrape out the cream from the cookies or just crush the entire cookie.)
4. Spoon the cookie crumbs into the bottom of your cup and pat them down. Layer the chocolate mixture on top. Finish with whipped cream and either more chocolate chips or Oreo mixture. Store in the refrigerator until ready to serve.

Nutrition: 45g carbs 12g fats 5g protein

97. Deadly Chocolate Sin

Preparation Time: 12'

Servings: 12

Cooking Time: 10'

Ingredients

- 1-2 tablespoons butter for greasing or cooking spray
- 6 ounces semisweet chocolate
- 1 cup unsalted butter
- 1 teaspoon vanilla extract
- 4 eggs, at room temperature
- 4 egg yolks, at room temperature
- ½ cup brown sugar, firmly packed
- 6 tablespoons cornstarch
- 1 (10 ounces) package frozen raspberries in a heavy syrup, thawed
- 1-pint fresh raspberries
- 2 ounces bitter chocolate
- 12 triangular cookies or chocolate pieces
- 12 sprigs fresh mint

Directions

1. Preheat the oven to 375°F. Prepare 12 (4 ounces) ramekins by buttering or spraying them with non-stick cooking spray. Combine the chocolate, unsalted butter, and vanilla in a double boiler and melt the chocolate, stirring to combine. In a large mixing bowl, beat together the eggs, egg yolks, and brown sugar. Mix this on high for 5–7 minutes, or until the volume almost doubles.
2. Set the mixer to low and add the cornstarch one tablespoon at a time, beating after each addition. Turn the mixer back to high and beat another 5 minutes or until soft peaks form.
3. Now, fold the chocolate into the egg mixture, making sure to scrape the bottom and sides of the bowl.
4. Pour the batter into the prepared ramekins and bake for 10 minutes. After 10 minutes, remove the ramekins from the oven and allow them to cool. Store in the refrigerator, covered with plastic wrap, until ready to serve.
5. When ready to serve, run a knife around the edges to loosen the cake, then invert the cake on serving plates.
6. Purée the thawed raspberries in a blender, then ladle them over the top of each cake. Top with fresh raspberries, chocolate pieces, and mint. Serve

Nutrition: 40g carbs 10g fats 6g protein

98. Orange Creamsicle Cake

Preparation Time: 30'

Servings: 8-10

Cooking Time: 30-35'

Ingredients

- 1 (18.25 ounce) box orange cake mix
- 1 (3 ounces) package orange-flavored gelatin
- 1 cup boiling water
- 1 (3.4 ounces) package instant vanilla pudding mix
- 1 cup milk
- 1 teaspoon vanilla extract
- 1 teaspoon orange extract
- 1 (8 ounces) tub Cool Whip®, thawed
- White chocolate shavings, to garnish

Directions

1. Preheat the oven to 350°F and prepare two 9-inch round cake pans by greasing and dusting them with flour. In a large bowl, prepare the packaged cake mix according to the package Directions. Divide the batter evenly between the prepared cake pans.
2. Bake for 35–45 minutes or until a toothpick inserted in the center comes out clean. Remove the cakes from the oven. While they are still hot, use the handle end of a wooden spoon to poke holes throughout.
3. Prepare the gelatin with one cup of hot water, and when it is dissolved completely, pour it over the hot cake, making sure the gelatin goes into all the holes.
4. Let the cake sit and cool completely. (You can put it in the refrigerator to speed up the process if you like.) Prepare the vanilla pudding using only one cup of milk. Fold in the Cool Whip, making sure it is well incorporated.
5. Put a layer of the pudding mixture between the cake layers and use the remaining to completely frost the cake. Garnish with chocolate shavings and grated orange peel if desired. Refrigerate until ready to serve.

Nutrition: 41g carbs 12g fats 3g protein

99. Cinnamon Apple Turnover

Preparation Time: 10'

Servings: 4-6

Cooking Time: 25'

Ingredients

- 1 large Granny Smith apple, peeled, cored, and diced
- ½ teaspoon cornstarch
- ¼ teaspoon cinnamon
- Dash ground nutmeg
- ¼ cup brown sugar
- ¼ cup applesauce
- ¼ teaspoon vanilla extract
- 1 tablespoon butter, melted
- 1 sheet of puff pastry, thawed
- Whipped cream or vanilla ice cream, to serve

Directions

1. Preheat the oven to 400°F. Prepare a baking sheet by spraying it with non-stick cooking spray or using a bit of oil on a paper towel.
2. In a mixing bowl, mix together the apples, cornstarch, cinnamon, nutmeg, and brown sugar. Stir to make sure the apples are well covered with the spices. Then stir in the applesauce and the vanilla.
3. Lay out your puff pastry and cut it into squares. You should be able to make 4 or 6 depending on how big you want your turnovers to be and how big your pastry is.
4. Place some of the apple mixture in the center of each square and fold the corners of the pastry up to make a pocket. Pinch the edges together to seal. Then brush a bit of the melted butter over the top to give the turnovers that nice brown color.
5. Place the filled pastry onto the prepared baking pan and transfer to the preheated oven. Bake 20–25 minutes, or until they become a golden brown in color. Serve with whipped cream or vanilla ice cream.

Nutrition: 43g carbs 13g fats 4g protein

100. Burger King's Hershey's Sundae Pie

Preparation Time: 20'

Servings: 8

Cooking Time: 10'

Ingredients

Crust
- 1½ cups crushed chocolate wafers
- 2 tablespoons sugar
- ½ cup melted butter

Cream cheese layer
- 8 ounces cream cheese
- ¾ cup powdered sugar
- 8 ounces Cool Whip or cream, plus more for topping
- 1 teaspoon vanilla extract

Chocolate layer
- 1 (3½-ounce) box chocolate pudding
- 1½ cups milk
- Chocolate syrup, for drizzling
- Chocolate chips, for topping

Directions

1. Preheat oven to 350°F. Meanwhile, prepare the crust. Place ingredients in a food processor or blender and pulse until well-blended. Spread and press into a 9-inch pie pan. Bake until fragrant and set (about 10 minutes). Place on a wire rack to cool.
2. Prepare the cream cheese layer. Beat the cream cheese until softened. Beat in sugar, Cool Whip, and vanilla until well-blended. Spread evenly over cooled crust.
3. Use 1½ cups milk to prepare pudding (follow packaging instructions) and spread over cream filling.
4. Top with dollops of Cool Whip, drizzle with chocolate syrup and sprinkle with chocolate chips.
5. Let chill to set.

Nutrition: 420 Calories 27.8g Total Fat 39.1g Carbs 5.2g Protein

101. Chili's Chocolate Brownie Sundae

Preparation Time: 20'

Servings: 8

Cooking Time: 30'

Ingredients

- ½ cup flour
- 1/3 cup cocoa
- ¼ teaspoon salt
- ¼ teaspoon baking powder
- ½ cup margarine, melted
- 1 cup white sugar
- 2 eggs
- 1 teaspoon vanilla
- ½ cup chocolate chips
- ½ gallon vanilla ice cream, slightly softened
- 1 (6-ounce) jar fudge topping
- Whipped cream, for topping (optional)
- ½ cup walnuts, coarsely chopped
- 8 maraschino cherries, for garnish

Directions

1. Preheat oven to 350°F. Grease a 9×9 baking pan. Sift together flour, cocoa, baking powder, and salt in a bowl. Set aside.
2. Combine melted margarine, sugar, eggs, and vanilla, blending well. Add flour mixture, stirring briefly to moisten. Stir in chocolate chips. Do not over-mix.
3. Pour into prepared pan. Bake until fragrant and corners begin to separate from the pan (about 30 minutes). If over-baked, the result will be cakey instead of fudgy.
4. Cool slightly before cutting into 8 bars. Place a scoop of ice cream on top of each brownie and drizzle with fudge sauce. Top with whipped cream (optional) and sprinkle with chopped walnuts.
5. Garnish with cherries.

Nutrition: 1290 Calories 61g Total Fat 195g Carbs 14g Protein

102. Ben & Jerry's Cherry Garcia Ice Cream

Preparation Time: 4 H

Servings: 4-8

Cooking Time: 0'

Ingredients

- ¼ cup Bing cherries, fresh or frozen (thawed), drained well and roughly chopped
- 2 cups thick cream
- 1 cup milk
- ¾ cup sugar
- 2 large eggs
- 1½ teaspoons vanilla extract (optional)
- ¼ cup semisweet chocolate, broken into bits

Directions

1. Chill cherries until ready for use. In a saucepan, whisk together cream, milk, sugar, and eggs. Whisk while heating gently to 165°F. Remove from heat. Strain into a bowl. Cover and let chill for about 2 hours. Place in ice cream maker and let churn. It should be ready in about 20 minutes. Add cherries and chocolate just before the ice cream is done. Transfer to containers, cover, and freeze well (about 4 hours). Serve and enjoy.

Nutrition: 250 Calories 14g Total Fat 26g Carbs 4g Protein

103. P.F. Chang's Coconut Pineapple Ice Cream with Banana Spring Rolls

| Preparation Time: | 5' | Servings: | 6 |

| Cooking Time: | 30' |

Ingredients

Ice Cream
- 1 (13½-ounce) can coconut milk
- 1 cup granulated sugar
- 1½ cups heavy cream
- 1 teaspoon coconut extract
- 1 (8-ounce) can crushed pineapple, drained
- 1/3 cup shredded coconut

Banana Spring Rolls
- 3 ripe bananas (preferably plantains), halved horizontally
- 3 rice paper or wonton wrappers
- 1–3 tablespoons brown sugar
- 1 teaspoon cinnamon
- Oil, for frying
- Caramel sauce, for drizzling (optional)
- Paste for sealing wrappers
- 2 tablespoons water
- 2 teaspoons flour or cornstarch

Directions

1. Make the ice cream. Place coconut milk and sugar in a mixing bowl. Mix with an electric mixer until sugar is dissolved. Mix in remaining ingredients until well-blended. Place in ice cream maker to churn (follow manufacturer's instructions) until ice cream holds when scooped with a spoon (about 30 minutes). Transfer to a container with lid and freeze for at least 2 hours or until desired firmness is reached.
2. Make the banana spring rolls. Lay the wrapper on a flat surface. Position a banana slice near the edge of the wrapper closest to you (the bottom). Sprinkle with about 1 teaspoon to 1 tablespoon brown sugar, depending on how sweet you want it. Sprinkle with a pinch or two of cinnamon. Roll up like a burrito, tucking in the sides. In a small bowl, stir the paste ingredients together. Brush the paste on the edge of the wrapper and seal the roll. Place roll, sealed side down, on a plate, and repeat with the remaining bananas. Heat oil, about 1–1½ inches deep, over medium to high heat. Fry the rolls until golden brown (1–2 minutes on each side). Place on paper towels to drain.
3. Serve the rolls with scoops of ice cream and drizzle with caramel sauce, if desired.

Nutrition: 146 Calories 11g Total Fat 33g Carbs 5g Protein

104. TGI Friday's Oreo Madness

| Preparation Time: | 10' + 2H FREEZING TIME | Servings: | 18 |

Cooking Time: 0'

Ingredients

- 1 (14-ounce) package Oreo cookies
- ½ cup (1 stick) butter, melted
- 5 cups vanilla ice cream
- For drizzling:
- Hot fudge and caramel toppings

Directions

1. Line muffin pans with cupcake liners. If needed, let ice cream stand at room temperature to soften a little for easier spreading. Place Oreos in a blender or food processor and pulse to break into crumbs.
2. Transfer to a bowl and stir in melted butter. Mix well. Press about 2 tablespoons each of crumb mixture into muffin tins. Top each with about ¼ cup ice cream, smoothening down with a spatula.
3. Cover with another 2 tablespoons of crumbs. Cover and freeze until set (about 2 hours). Remove from muffin tins. Drizzle with toppings and serve.

Nutrition: 287 Calories 14g Total Fat 38.1g Carbs 2.6g Protein

105. Ben & Jerry's Chunky Monkey Ice Cream

| Preparation Time: | 20' + 8H FREEZING TIME | Servings: | 4-8 |

| Cooking Time: | 30' |

Ingredients

- 3 medium ripe bananas, peeled and cut into bite-size pieces
- ☐ cup brown sugar, packed
- 1 tablespoon butter, diced
- 1½ cups whole milk
- 2 tablespoons granulated sugar
- ½ teaspoon vanilla extract
- 1½ teaspoons freshly-squeezed lemon juice
- ¼ teaspoon coarse or sea salt
- ¼ cup walnuts, coarsely chopped
- ¼ cup chopped dark chocolate or dark chocolate chips

Directions

1. Preheat oven or oven-type toaster to 400°F. In a shallow baking dish, coat the banana slices with brown sugar and sprinkle with butter.
2. Bake until sugar is caramelized, and bananas are browned (about 30–40 minutes), stirring occasionally. Let cool slightly and then combine with milk, sugar, vanilla, lemon juice, and salt.
3. Use a blender or food processor to make a smooth puree. Cover with plastic wrap and chill for about 4 hours. Transfer to ice cream maker and let churn, following manufacturer's instructions.
4. Stir in walnuts and chocolate. Freeze for about 4 hours or until of desired consistency.

Nutrition: 290 Calories 17g Total Fat 30g Carbs 4g Protein

106. Jack in the Box's Oreo Cookie Shake

Preparation Time: 5'

Servings: 2

Cooking Time: 0'

Ingredients

- 3 cups vanilla ice cream
- 1½ cups milk, cold
- 8 Oreo cookies, without filling, broken into small pieces
- Whipped cream, for topping (optional)
- 2 cherries, for garnish (optional)

Directions

1. Place ice cream and milk in a blender. Pulse gently until smooth. Continue blending at low speed and add Oreos. Blend until cookies are pureed (about 10 seconds). Pour into 2 cups or glasses. Top with whipped cream and cherries (optional).

Nutrition: 722 Calories 36.4g Total Fat 83.7g Carbs 18.7g Protein

107. Dairy Queen's Candy Cane Chill

Preparation Time: 5'	**Servings:** 2

Cooking Time: 0'

Ingredients

- 4 large scoops vanilla ice cream
- 1 cup Cool Whip, thawed or frozen
- ¼ cup milk
- 3 regular sized candy canes, broken into small pieces
- ¼ cup chocolate chunks

Directions

1. Place all ingredients in a blender. Blend to desired consistency. (Add more ice cream, if needed.) Pour into 2 glasses or mugs.

Nutrition: 536 Calories 26.6g Total Fat 68.5g Carbs 6.6g Protein

108. Dairy Queen's Blizzard

Preparation Time: 5'

Servings: 1

Cooking Time: 0'

Ingredients

- 1 candy bar, of your choice
- ¼ to ½ cup milk
- 2½ cups vanilla ice cream
- 1 teaspoon fudge sauce

Directions

1. Place the candy bar of your choice into the freezer to harden it. Break the candy bar into multiple tiny chunks and place all the ingredients into a blender.
2. Keep blending until the ice cream becomes thicker, and everything is mixed completely.
3. Pour into a cup and consume.

Nutrition: 953 Calories 51.6g Total Fat 108.8g Carbs 15.1g Protein

109. Applebee's Maple Butter Blondie

Preparation Time: 10'

Servings: 6

Cooking Time: 25'

Ingredients

- 1/3 cup butter, melted
- 1 cup brown sugar, packed
- 1 egg, beaten
- 1 tablespoon vanilla extract
- 1 cup all-purpose flour
- ½ teaspoon baking powder
- 1/8 teaspoon baking soda
- 1/8 teaspoon salt
- ½ cup white chocolate chips
- ½ cup walnuts or pecans, chopped

Maple Cream Sauce:
- ½ cup maple syrup
- ¼ cup butter
- ½ cup brown sugar
- 8 ounces cream cheese, softened
- Walnuts for garnish, chopped; optional
- Vanilla ice cream for serving

Directions

1. Preheating the oven to 350F, and Greasing an 8×8 baking pan.
2. Dissolve the sugar in the melted butter. Whip in the egg and the vanilla and set the mixture aside.
3. In another bowl, mix together the flour, baking powder and soda, and salt.
4. Slowly pour the dry mixture into the butter mixture and mix thoroughly.
5. Make sure the mixture is at room temperature before folding in the nuts and chocolate chips.
6. Transfer the mixture into the baking pan and bake for 20 to 25 minutes.
7. While waiting for the blondies to bake, combine the syrup and butter over low heat. When the butter has melted, mix in the sugar and cream cheese. Take the mixture off the heat when the cream cheese has melted and set aside.
8. Let the blondies cool a little and then cut them into rectangles. Serve with the syrup, top with walnuts and vanilla ice cream, if desired, and serve.

Nutrition: 1000 Calories 54g Total Fat 117g Carbs 13g Protein

110. Houston's Apple Walnut Cobbler

Preparation Time: 15'

Servings: 6

Cooking Time: 30'

Ingredients

- 3 large Granny Smith apples, peeled and diced
- 1½ cups walnuts, coarsely chopped
- 1 cup all-purpose flour
- 1 cup brown sugar
- 1 teaspoon cinnamon
- Pinch of nutmeg (optional)
- 1 large egg
- ½ cup (1 stick) butter, melted
- Vanilla ice cream
- Caramel sauce, for drizzling (optional)

Directions

1. Preheat oven to 350°F. Lightly grease an 8-inch square baking dish. Spread diced apple over the bottom of the baking dish. Sprinkle with walnuts.
2. In a bowl, mix together flour, sugar, cinnamon, nutmeg (optional), and egg to make a coarse-textured mixture. Sprinkle over the apple-walnut layer.
3. Pour melted butter over the whole mixture. Bake until fragrant and crumb top is browned (about 30 minutes). Serve warm topped with scoops of vanilla ice cream. Drizzle with caramel sauce (optional).

Nutrition: 611 Calories 36g Total Fat 69g Carbs 8g Protein

111. Melting Pot Chocolate Fondue

Preparation Time: 10'

Servings: 4

Cooking Time: 5'

Ingredients

- 8 ounces semi-sweet or dark chocolate chips
- 1 cup heavy cream
- 1 tablespoon unsalted butter
- 2 tablespoons chunky peanut butter or Nutella (optional)
- Possible complements: strawberry, banana, grapes, cherries, brownies, cream puffs, rice puffs, marshmallows, or cheesecake, cut into bite-size pieces

Directions

1. Heat cream in a saucepan to a simmer. Stir in butter, chocolate, and peanut butter or Nutella (if using). Let sit to allow the chocolate to melt (about 2 minutes). Whisk until smooth and serve immediately with desired complements.

Nutrition: 667 Calories 32g Total Fat 84g Carbs 9g Protein

112. P.F. Chang's Ginger Panna Cotta

Preparation Time: 10'

Servings: 3

Cooking Time: 4H 10'

Ingredients

Panna Cotta:
- ¼ cup heavy cream
- ½ cup granulated sugar
- 1 tablespoon grated ginger
- 1½ tablespoons powdered gelatin
- 6 tablespoons warm water

Strawberry Sauce:
- 2 pounds ripe strawberries, hulled
- ½ cup granulated sugar
- 2 teaspoons cornstarch
- ½ lemon, juice
- 1 pinch salt

Directions

1. Place the cream, sugar, and ginger in a saucepan and cook over medium-low heat, until the sugar dissolves. Remove the mixture from heat and set aside.
2. In a medium-sized bowl, mix the water and the gelatin together. Set aside for a few minutes. After the gelatin has rested, pour the sugar mixture into the medium-sized bowl and stir, removing all lumps.
3. Grease your ramekins and then transfer the mixture into the ramekins, leaving 2 inches of space at the top.
4. Place the ramekins in your refrigerator or freezer to let them set for at least 4 hours.
5. While the panna cottas are setting, make the strawberry sauce by cooking all the sauce ingredients in a medium-sized pan for 10 minutes. Stir the mixture occasionally, then remove from heat.
6. When the panna cottas are ready, flip over the containers onto a plate and allow the gelatin to stand. Drizzle with the strawberry sauce and serve.

Nutrition: 346 Calories 30g Total Fat 16g Carbs 4g Protein

113. Starbucks' Cranberry Bliss Bars

Preparation Time: 35'

Servings: 6

Cooking Time: 20'

Ingredients

- 2¼ cups all-purpose flour
- 1½ teaspoons baking powder
- ¼ teaspoon salt
- 1/8 teaspoon ground cinnamon
- ¾ cup butter, melted
- 1½ cups light brown sugar, packed
- 2 large eggs
- ¾ teaspoon vanilla extract
- ½ cup dried cranberries
- 6 ounces white baking chocolate, coarsely chopped
- White Chocolate Frosting
- 1 (8-ounce) package cream cheese, cubed, softened
- 1 cup powdered sugar
- 1 tablespoon grated orange zest, or to taste
- 6 ounces white baking chocolate, melted, divided
- ½ cup dried cranberries, chopped

Directions

1. Preheat oven to 350°F. Grease a 9×13-inch baking pan. In a bowl, combine flour, baking powder, salt, and cinnamon. Set aside. In a mixer bowl, combine the still-warm melted butter with sugar. Let cool slightly.
2. While mixing continuously, add eggs one at a time. Mix in vanilla. Add flour mixture and mix to incorporate and to make a thick batter. Stir in cranberries and chopped chocolate.
3. Spread evenly in prepared pan. Bake until the toothpick inserted in the center comes out clean (about 18–20 minutes). Let cool completely on a wire rack.
4. Meanwhile, prepare the frosting. Beat cream cheese, powdered sugar, and orange zest until well-blended. Gradually add half of the melted white chocolate and mix until smooth.
5. Spread the frosting over the cooled blondies. Sprinkle with cranberries and drizzle with the remaining melted chocolate. Cut into bars or triangles and serve.

Nutrition: 198 Calories 8g Total Fat 28g Carbs 2g Protein

114. Olive Garden's Tiramisu

Preparation Time: 10'

Servings: 9

Cooking Time: 2 H 40'

Ingredients

- 4 egg yolks
- 2 tablespoons milk
- 2/3 cup granulated sugar
- 2 cups mascarpone cheese
- ¼ teaspoon vanilla extract
- 1 cup heavy cream
- ½ cup cold espresso
- ¼ cup Kahlua
- 20–24 ladyfingers
- 2 teaspoons cocoa powder

Directions

1. Bring water to a boil, then reduce the heat to maintain a simmer. Place a heatproof bowl over the water, making sure that the bowl does not touch the water. In the heatproof bowl, whisk together the egg yolks, milk, and sugar for about 8 to 10 minutes.
2. When the mixture has thickened, remove the bowl from heat and then whisk in the vanilla and mascarpone cheese until the mixture becomes smooth. In another bowl, whisk the cream until soft peaks are formed.
3. Using a spatula, fold the whipped cream into the mascarpone mixture, making sure to retain the fluffiness of the whipped cream. In another bowl, mix the espresso and Kahlua.
4. Dip the ladyfingers into the espresso mixture one by one. Dip only the bottom, and dip them quickly so as not to make them soggy. Cover the bottom of an 8×8 pan with half of the dipped ladyfingers, cracking them if necessary.
5. Pour half of the mascarpone mixture over the ladyfingers. Place another layer of ladyfingers over the mixture. Pour the rest of the mixture over the second layer of ladyfingers and smooth out the top.
6. Dust some cocoa powder over the top and then place it in the refrigerator. Slice the cake and serve when set.

Nutrition: 289 Calories 14g Total Fat 34.4g Carbs 4g Protein

115. Maple Butter Blondie

Preparation Time: 15'

Servings: 9

Cooking Time: 35'

Ingredients

- 1/3 cup butter, melted
- 1 cup brown sugar, packed
- 1 large egg, beaten
- 1 tablespoon vanilla extract
- ½ teaspoon baking powder
- 1/8 teaspoon baking soda
- 1/8 teaspoon salt
- 1 cup flour
- 2/3 cup white chocolate chips
- 1/3 cup pecans, chopped (or walnuts)
- Maple butter sauce
- ¾ cup maple syrup
- ½ cup butter
- ¾ cup brown sugar
- 8 ounces cream cheese, softened to room temp
- ¼ cup pecans, chopped
- Vanilla ice cream, for serving

Directions

1. Preheat the oven to 350°F and coat a 9x9 baking pan with cooking spray. In a mixing bowl, combine the butter, brown sugar, egg, and vanilla, and beat until smooth.
2. Sift in the baking powder, baking soda, salt, and flour, and stir until it is well incorporated. Fold in the white chocolate chips. Bake for 20–25 minutes.
3. While those are in the oven, prepare the maple butter sauce by combining the maple syrup and butter in a medium saucepan.
4. Cook over low heat until the butter is melted. Add the brown sugar and cream cheese. Stir constantly until the cream cheese has completely melted, then remove the pot from the heat.
5. Remove the blondies from the oven and cut them into squares. Top with vanilla ice cream, maple butter sauce, and chopped nuts.

Nutrition: 40g carbs 12g fats 4g protein

116. Chef John's Zabaglione

Preparation Time: 10'

Servings: 2

Cooking Time: 1H 25'

Ingredients

- ½ cup Strawberries
- 3 tbsp and 1 tsp White sugar
- 3 Egg yolks
- ¼ cup Dry Marsala wine

Directions

1. Remove the hulls, slice the strawberries into halves, and mix them with the sugar (1 tsp.). Cover the bowl and let it rest on the countertop for about one hour. Portion fruit into two serving bowls of choice.
2. Toss the yolks of the eggs, sugar, and marsala into a metal mixing container. Heat it using the low-temperature setting. As it heats, whisk until it forms loose peaks (6-8 min.) and warm to the touch.
3. Scoop the custard over the berries and serve warm.

Nutrition: 44g carbs 11g fats 5g protein

117. Chocolate Mousse Dessert Shooter

| Preparation Time: | 30' | Servings: | 4 |

Cooking Time: 0'

Ingredients

- 2 tablespoons butter
- 6 ounces semi-sweet chocolate chips (1 cup), divided
- 2 eggs
- 1 teaspoon vanilla
- 8 Oreo® cookies
- ½ cup prepared fudge sauce
- 2 tablespoons sugar
- ½ cup heavy cream
- Canned whipped cream

Directions

1. Melt the butter and all but 1 tablespoon of the chocolate chips in a double boiler.
2. When they are melted, stir in the vanilla and remove from the heat.
3. Whisk in the egg yolks.
4. Beat the egg whites until they form soft peaks, and then fold them into the chocolate mixture.
5. Beat the sugar and heavy cream in a separate bowl until it forms stiff peaks or is the consistency that you desire. Fold this into the chocolate mixture.
6. Crush the remaining chocolate chips into small pieces and stir them into the chocolate. Crush the Oreos. (You can either scrape out the cream from the cookies or just crush the entire cookie.)
7. Spoon the cookie crumbs into the bottom of your cup and pat them down. Layer the chocolate mixture on top. Finish with whipped cream and either more chocolate chips or Oreo mixture.
8. Store in the refrigerator until ready to serve.

Nutrition: 41g carbs 12g fats 2g protein

118. Cinnamon Apple Turnover

| Preparation Time: | 10' | Servings: | 4-6 |

| Cooking Time: | 25' |

Ingredients

- 1 large Granny Smith apple, peeled, cored, and diced
- ½ teaspoon cornstarch
- ¼ teaspoon cinnamon
- Dash ground nutmeg
- ¼ cup brown sugar
- ¼ cup applesauce
- ¼ teaspoon vanilla extract
- 1 tablespoon butter, melted
- 1 sheet of puff pastry, thawed
- Whipped cream or vanilla ice cream, to serve

Directions

1. Preheat the oven to 400°F. Prepare a baking sheet by spraying it with non-stick cooking spray or using a bit of oil on a paper towel.
2. In a mixing bowl, mix together the apples, cornstarch, cinnamon, nutmeg, and brown sugar. Stir to make sure the apples are well covered with the spices. Then stir in the applesauce and the vanilla.
3. Lay out your puff pastry and cut it into squares. You should be able to make 4 or 6 depending on how big you want your turnovers to be and how big your pastry is.
4. Place some of the apple mixture in the center of each square and fold the corners of the pastry up to make a pocket. Pinch the edges together to seal. Then brush a bit of the melted butter over the top to give the turnovers that nice brown color.
5. Place the filled pastry onto the prepared baking pan and transfer to the preheated oven. Bake 20–25 minutes, or until they become a golden brown in color. Serve with whipped cream or vanilla ice cream.

Nutrition: 42g carbs 13g fats 4g protein

119. Cherry Chocolate Cobbler

Preparation Time: 10'

Servings: 8

Cooking Time: 45'

Ingredients

- 1½ cups all-purpose flour
- ½ cup sugar
- 2 teaspoons baking powder
- ½ teaspoon salt
- ¼ cup butter
- 6 ounces semisweet chocolate morsels
- ¼ cup milk
- 1 egg, beaten
- 21 ounces cherry pie filling
- ½ cup finely chopped nuts

Directions

1. Preheat the oven to 350°F. Combine the flour, sugar, baking powder, salt, and butter in a large mixing bowl. Use a pastry blender to cut the mixture until there are lumps the size of small peas.
2. Melt the chocolate morsels. Let cool for approximately 5 minutes, then add the milk and egg and mix well. Beat into the flour mixture, mixing completely. Spread the pie filling in a 2-quart casserole dish. Randomly drop the chocolate batter over the filling, then sprinkle with nuts.
3. Bake for 40–45 minutes. Serve with a scoop of vanilla ice cream if desired.

Nutrition: 45g carbs 14g fats 3g protein

120. Pumpkin Custard with Gingersnaps

Preparation Time: 30'

Servings: 8

Cooking Time: 35'

Ingredients

Custard
- 8 egg yolks
- 1¾ cups (1 15-ounce can) pure pumpkin puree
- 1¾ cups heavy whipping cream
- ½ cup sugar
- 1½ teaspoons pumpkin pie spice
- 1 teaspoon vanilla

Topping
- 1 cup crushed gingersnap cookies
- 1 tablespoon melted butter

Whipped Cream
- 1 cup heavy whipping cream
- 1 tablespoon superfine sugar (or regular sugar if you have no caster sugar)
- ½ teaspoon pumpkin pie spice

Garnish
- 8 whole gingersnap cookies

Directions

1. Preheat the oven to 350°F. Separate the yolks from 8 eggs and whisk them together in a large mixing bowl until they are well blended and creamy.
2. Add the pumpkin, sugar, vanilla, heavy cream, and pumpkin pie spice and whisk to combine. Cook the custard mixture in a double boiler, stirring until it has thickened enough that it coats a spoon.
3. Pour the mixture into individual custard cups or an 8×8-inch baking pan and bake for about 20 minutes if using individual cups or 30–35 minutes for the baking pan, until it is set and a knife inserted comes out clean.
4. While the custard is baking, make the topping by combining the crushed gingersnaps and melted butter. After the custard has been in the oven for 15 minutes, sprinkle the gingersnap mixture over the top.
5. When the custard has passed the clean knife test, remove from the oven, and let cool to room temperature. Whisk the heavy cream and pumpkin pie spice together with the caster sugar and beat just until it thickens. Serve the custard with the whipped cream and garnish each serving with a gingersnap.

Nutrition: 44g carbs 14g fats 3g protein

121. Baked Apple Dumplings

Preparation Time: 20'

Servings: 2-4

Cooking Time: 40'

Ingredients

- 1 (17½ ounce) package frozen puff pastry, thawed
- 1 cup sugar
- 6 tablespoons dry breadcrumbs
- 2 teaspoons ground cinnamon
- 1 pinch ground nutmeg
- 1 egg, beaten
- 4 Granny Smith apples, peeled, cored, and halved
- Vanilla ice cream for serving

Icing
- 1 cup confectioners' sugar
- 1 teaspoon vanilla extract
- 3 tablespoons milk

Pecan Streusel
- 2/3 cup chopped toasted pecans
- 2/3 cup packed brown sugar
- 2/3 cup all-purpose flour
- 5 tablespoons melted butter

Directions

1. Preheat the oven to 425°F. When the puff pastry has completely thawed, roll out each sheet to measure 12 inches by 12 inches. Cut the sheets into quarters. Combine the sugar, breadcrumbs, cinnamon, and nutmeg together in a small bowl.
2. Brush one of the pastry squares with some of the beaten egg. Add about 1 tablespoon of the breadcrumb mixture on top, then add half an apple, core side down, over the crumbs. Add another tablespoon of the breadcrumb mixture.
3. Seal the dumpling by pulling up the corners and pinching the pastry together until the seams are totally sealed. Repeat this process with the remaining squares. Assemble the ingredients for the pecan streusel in a small bowl.
4. Grease a baking sheet or line it with parchment paper. Place the dumplings on the sheet and brush them with a bit more of the beaten egg. Top with the pecan streusel.
5. Bake for 15 minutes, then reduce heat to 350°F and bake for 25 minutes more or until lightly browned. Make the icing by combining the confectioners' sugar, vanilla, and milk until you reach the proper consistency.
6. When the dumplings are done, let them cool to room temperature and drizzle them with icing before serving.

Nutrition: 43g carbs 13g fats 3.1g protein

122. Peach Cobbler

Preparation Time: 10'

Servings: 4

Cooking Time: 45'

Ingredients

- 1¼ cups Bisquick
- 1 cup milk
- ½ cup melted butter
- ¼ teaspoon nutmeg
- ½ teaspoon cinnamon
- Vanilla ice cream, for serving

Filling
- 1 (30-ounce) can peaches in syrup, drained
- ¼ cup sugar

Topping
- ½ cup brown sugar
- ¼ cup almond slices
- ½ teaspoon cinnamon
- 1 tablespoon melted butter

Directions

1. Preheat the oven to 375°F. Grease the bottom and sides of an 8×8-inch pan. Whisk together the Bisquick, milk, butter, nutmeg, and cinnamon in a large mixing bowl. When thoroughly combined, pour into the greased baking pan.
2. Mix together the peaches and sugar in another mixing bowl. Put the filling on top of the batter in the pan. Bake for about 45 minutes.
3. In another bowl, mix together the brown sugar, almonds, cinnamon, and melted butter. After the cobbler has cooked for 45 minutes, cover evenly with the topping and bake for an additional 10 minutes. Serve with a scoop of vanilla ice cream.

Nutrition: 41g carbs 13g fats 4g protein

123. Campfire S'mores

Preparation Time: 15'

Servings: 9

Cooking Time: 40'

Ingredients

Graham Cracker Crust
- 2 cups graham cracker crumbs
- ¼ cup sugar
- ½ cup butter
- ½ teaspoon cinnamon
- 1 small package brownie mix (enough for an 8×8-inch pan)

Brownie Mix
- ½ cup flour
- 1/3 cup cocoa
- ¼ teaspoon baking powder
- ¼ teaspoon salt
- ½ cup butter
- 1 cup sugar
- 1 teaspoon vanilla
- 2 large eggs

S'mores Topping
- 9 large marshmallows
- 5 Hershey candy bars
- 4½ cups vanilla ice cream
- ½ cup chocolate sauce

Directions

1. Preheat the oven to 350°F.
2. Mix together the graham cracker crumbs, sugar, cinnamon, and melted butter in a medium bowl. Stir until the crumbs and sugar have combined with the butter.
3. Line an 8×8-inch baking dish with parchment paper. Make sure to use enough so that you'll be able to lift the baked brownies out of the dish easily. Press the graham cracker mixture into the bottom of the lined pan.
4. Place the pan in the oven to prebake the crust a bit while you are making the brownie mixture.
5. Melt the butter over medium heat in a large saucepan, then stir in the sugar and vanilla. Whisk in the eggs one at a time. Then whisk in the dry ingredients, followed by the nuts. Mix until smooth. Take the crust out of the oven, pour the mixture into it, and bake for 23–25 minutes. When brownies are done, remove from oven and let cool in the pan.
6. After the brownies have cooled completely, lift them out of the pan using the edges of the parchment paper. Be careful not to crack or break the brownies. Cut into individual slices.
7. When you are ready to serve, place a marshmallow on top of each brownie and broil in the oven until the marshmallow starts to brown. You can also microwave for a couple of seconds, but you won't get the browning that you would in the broiler.
8. Remove from the oven and top each brownie with half of a Hershey bar. Serve with ice cream and a drizzle of chocolate sauce.

Nutrition: 41g carbs 12g fats 4g protein

124. Banana Pudding

Preparation Time: 15' + 1H 30' CHILLING TIME

Servings: 8-10

Cooking Time: 0'

Ingredients

- 6 cups milk
- 5 eggs, beaten
- ¼ teaspoon vanilla extract
- 11/8 cups flour
- 1½ cups sugar
- ¾ pound vanilla wafers
- 3 bananas, peeled
- 8 ounces whipped cream

Directions

1. In a large saucepan, heat the milk to about 170°F.
2. Mix the eggs, vanilla, flour, and sugar together in a large bowl. Very slowly add the egg mixture to the warmed milk and cook until the mixture thickens to a custard consistency.
3. Layer the vanilla wafers to cover the bottom of a baking pan or glass baking dish. You can also use individual portion dessert dish or glasses.
4. Layer banana slices over the top of the vanilla wafers. Be as liberal with the bananas as you want.
5. Layer the custard mixture on top of the wafers and bananas. Move the pan to the refrigerator and cool for 1½ hours. When ready to serve, spread Cool Whip (or real whipped cream, if you prefer) over the top. Garnish with banana slices and wafers if desired.

Nutrition: 45g carbs 14g fats 3g protein

125. Chili's New York Style Cheesecake

Preparation Time: 35'

Servings: 12

Cooking Time: 1H 25'

Ingredients

- 15 graham crackers (each 3 by 5"), broken into pieces
- 2 ½ pounds cream cheese (five 8-ounce bars), room temperature
- 1 teaspoon packed lemon zest, finely grated plus 1 tablespoon fresh juice
- 1/3 cup dark-brown sugar, packed
- 1 1/3 cups granulated sugar
- 1 cup sour cream, at room temperature
- 5 large eggs, at room temperature
- 1 ¼ teaspoons coarse salt
- 6 tablespoons softened butter, unsalted, melted, plus more for pan
- 1 teaspoon pure vanilla extract

Directions

1. Preheat oven to 350 F. Finely grind the crackers in a food processor. Add in the brown sugar, melted butter, zest & ½ teaspoon of salt; continue to pulse until you get wet sand-like texture. Evenly press into the bottom & halfway up sides of a buttered 9" spring form pan. Bake in the preheated oven for 12 to 15 minutes until set. Let cool.
2. Decrease your oven temperature to 325 F. Beat the cream cheese until smooth, on medium speed. Slowly beat in the granulated sugar for 2 to 3 minutes until light & fluffy. Beat in the lemon juice & leftover salt. Slowly beat in the eggs and then the vanilla and sour cream until completely smooth.
3. Place the pan in the middle of a double layer of foil. Lift the edges of foil up, tightly wrapping it around the sides of your pan & fold it in under itself until flush with the top of the pan.
4. Pour the filling into pan & smooth the top using a small offset spatula.
5. Place the springform pan in a roasting pan; transfer to the oven. Pour enough boiling water into the roasting pan to come halfway up sides of the springform pan. Bake in the preheated oven 1 hour 45 minutes to 2 hours until the cake is puffed & turn slightly wobbly in the center and golden brown on top.
6. Remove the springform pan from roasting pan; let cool for 20 minutes on a wire rack. Remove the foil and run a paring knife around the sides of the pan to loosen. Let completely cool. Drape the pan with a plastic wrap; refrigerate for overnight until cold. Remove the cake from pan; serve & enjoy.

Nutrition: 44g carbs 12g fats 3.9g protein

126. Starbuck's Copycat Cranberry Chocolate Bliss Bars

Preparation Time: 10'

Servings: 3 DOZEN

Cooking Time: 55'

Ingredients

- 3/4 cup of cubed butter, unsalted
- 1 1/2 cups of brown sugar, light, packed
- 2 eggs, large
- 3/4 tsp. of vanilla extract, pure
- 1 1/2 tsp. of baking powder
- 2 1/4 cups of flour, all-purpose
- 1/4 tsp. of salt, kosher
- 1/8 tsp. of cinnamon, ground
- 1/2 cup of cranberries, dried
- 6 oz. of chopped baking chocolate, white
- Frosting, 1 container prepared

Directions

1. Preheat the oven to 350F. In a large-sized microwave-safe bowl, melt butter. Add and stir in brown sugar. Cool a bit.
2. Beat in vanilla and eggs. In a separate bowl, whisk flour, kosher salt, cinnamon, and baking powder together. Stir in the chocolate and cranberries, making a thick batter. Spread into buttered 13" x 9" pan. Bake till golden brown, 18 to 20 minutes or so. Completely cool on wire rack. Slice and serve.

Nutrition: 42g carbs 13g fats 3.4g protein

127. Chocolate Pecan

Preparation Time: 10'

Servings: 8

Cooking Time: 50'

Ingredients

- 3 eggs
- ½ cup sugar
- 1 cup corn syrup
- ½ teaspoon salt
- 1 teaspoon vanilla extract
- ¼ cup melted butter
- 1 cup pecans
- 3 tablespoons semisweet chocolate chips
- 1 unbaked pie shell

Directions

1. Preheat the oven to 350°F. Beat together the eggs and sugar in a mixing bowl, then add the corn syrup, salt, vanilla, and butter. Put the chocolate chips and pecans inside the pie shell and pour the egg mixture over the top. Bake for 50–60 minutes or until set. Serve with vanilla ice cream.

Nutrition: 41.9g carbs 5.1g fats 3.1g protein

128. Peanut Butter Kisses

Preparation Time: 5'

Servings: 22

Cooking Time: 1 H 20'

Ingredients

- 1 ½ cups of smooth, unsweetened peanut butter
- 1 cup of coconut flour
- ¼ cup of keto sweetener (Swerve)
- a pinch of salt
- 1 tsp of vanilla extract
- 2 cups of dark chocolate
- 1 tbsp of coconut oil
- ¼ cup of nuts, chopped finely
- 4 tbsps. of peanut butter for drizzling

Directions

1. Place the 1 ½ cups of peanut butter in a microwave safe dish and heat it for about 15 seconds to melt.
2. Pour the peanut butter, coconut flour, sweetener, vanilla extract, and salt in a medium bowl and mix until a smooth, thick paste is formed.
3. Prepare a baking tray and line it with parchment paper (make sure that this tray can fit in your freezer).
4. Use an ice cream scoop (preferably) to scoop the peanut butter mixture and place dollops of small circles of the mixture onto the baking tray (you should have about 20 scoops' worth). Place the tray in the freezer and allow the mixture to freeze for about 1 hour until firm.
5. When the peanut butter balls are almost ready, place the dark chocolate in a microwave safe bowl and microwave the chocolate until it has melted, then allow it to cool to room temperature.
6. Add the melted chocolate into a medium bowl, along with the coconut oil and the chopped nuts. Place the remaining 4 tbsps. of peanut butter into a microwave safe bowl and melt the peanut butter.
7. When the peanut butter balls are firm, use a fork to dip the balls into the chocolate mixture and place them back on the baking tray. Drizzle the peanut butter over the balls. Place the tray back into the freezer for another 10 minutes and enjoy cold.

Nutrition: 259 Calories 19g Carbohydrates 18g Fat 8g Protein

129. Peanut Butter & Pecan Nut Cheesecake

Preparation Time: 30' + 4H CHILLING TIME

Servings: 10'

Cooking Time: 3 H

Ingredients

For the crust:
- 3 tbsps. of butter
- 1 ½ cups of pecan nuts
- 2 tbsps. of powdered erythritol
- 2 tbsps. of sultanas

For the filling:
- 12 tbsps. of butter
- 32 oz of cream cheese
- 1 cup of powdered erythritol
- ½ cup of whipping cream
- 4 teaspoons vanilla extract
- ½ tsp of cinnamon
- 4 eggs

For the topping:
- a handful of sultanas
- ¼ cup of crushed pecan nuts
- 1 tbsp of cinnamon
- 2 tbsps. of honey

Nutrition: 6g Calories 606 Carbohydrates 61g Fat 9g Protein

Directions

1. Preheat the oven to 325°F and prepare a springform/cake dish about 9" in size. Lightly grease the pan with a small dollop of butter.
2. Place the 3 tbsps. of butter into a small bowl and place it in the microwave for 10 seconds to melt the butter. Then set the butter aside to cool to room temperature.
3. Place the pecan nuts into a food processor and pulse until it's a fine, grounded texture.
4. Add the ground pecan nuts into the bowl with the melted butter, and pour the powdered erythritol and sultanas into the mixture. Mix the contents well in the bowl to combine the ingredients, then evenly pour the mixture into the base of the springform dish and use your fingers to firmly press in the pecan nut mixture. This should form a firm base with no cracks or spaces.
5. Place the crust in the oven for 10 minutes, then remove and set the dish aside to cool down. Keep the oven's temperature at 325°F as you'll be using it again soon.
6. For the filling, pour the remaining 12 tbsps of butter into a medium saucepan over medium-high heat and stir, while the butter melts. Once the butter has melted, and it starts to brown a little, remove it from the heat and set aside.
7. Pour the cream cheese into a medium bowl and slowly mix it to soften it, using a hand mixer. Once the cream cheese is soft and fluffy, add the remaining 1 cup of erythritol, heavy cream, cinnamon, and vanilla extract into the bowl and gently mix the ingredients together.
8. Crack the eggs into the bowl and then pour in the butter, while still slowly mixing to combine the ingredients, until well combined.
9. Use aluminum foil to wrap the sides and base of the springform pan, twice, then pour the filling into the pan, covering the base.
10. Place the springform pan on a baking tray and place it into the oven.
11. Pour water into the baking tray, so that it covers a few inches surrounding the springform pan.
12. Bake the cake for 1 hour and 10 minutes.
13. Remove the cake from the oven and the baking tray filled with water. Place the springform pan on a dry/cooling rack for 10 minutes, then use a spatula/butter knife to loosen the edges of the cake from the pan.
14. Separate the cake from the pan and allow the cake to cool for another hour at room temperature, then cover the cake with a lid/plastic wrap and place it in the refrigerator to set. This should preferably be left in the refrigerator overnight or for at least 4 hours to allow the cake to fully set.
15. When the cake has set, mix the honey and remaining cinnamon in a cup, stirring well to mix the ingredients. Lightly drizzle a loose design over the top of the cake with the honey mixture. Sprinkle the sultanas and crushed pecan nuts on top.

130. Three-Ingredient Chocolate Macadamia Fat Bombs

Preparation Time: 5'

Servings: 4

Cooking Time: 30'

Ingredients

- 1 ☐ oz of dark chocolate chips/dark chocolate shavings
- 1 ½ oz of macadamia nuts, halved
- 1 tbsp of coconut oil
- ½ tsp of cinnamon
- a pinch of salt

Directions

1. Prepare a tray that will work well for making truffles, i.e., a truffle mold or a mini muffin pan that has cup sizes of about 2x1" each. Make sure that this tray can also fit in your freezer.
2. In a microwave safe bowl, add the chocolate into the bowl and place it in the microwave for 30 seconds-1 minutes, until the chocolate has melted. Set the chocolate aside to cool down for a few seconds.
3. Add 3 macadamia nut halves into each cup (should be about 8 cups) and set aside. Return back to the bowl with the melted chocolate, and add in both the coconut oil and a pinch of salt and cinnamon, then mix until well combined.
4. Spoon the chocolate mixture evenly into each cup of the tray, covering the macadamia nut base.
5. Use the spoon to level out the surfaces of the cups and then place the tray in the freezer for 30-40 minutes until the chocolate has solidified.

Nutrition: 167 Calories 2g Carbohydrates 16g Fat 2g Protein

131. Goat Cheese with Stewed Blackberries

| Preparation Time: | 10' | Servings: | 4 |

| Cooking Time: | 12' |

Ingredients

- 20 oz of goat cheese
- 9 oz of blackberries
- 1 tbsp of erythritol
- ½ tsp of cinnamon
- 2 tbsps.' of paprika
- 1 mint leaf
- 1 oz of pistachio nuts
- 2 thin slices of orange

Directions

1. Preheat the oven to 350°F and prepare an oven tray.
2. In a microwave safe, small bowl, mix the blackberries, erythritol, 1 tbsp of water, and cinnamon together. Place the bowl in the microwave for 20-30 seconds to lightly warm the mixture. Stir the mixture once more. Slap the mint leaf to awaken the aromas and add the leaf into the bowl. Cover the bowl and set it aside, allowing the flavors to infuse together.
3. Place the goat cheese on the baking tray and place it in the oven to bake for about 10 minutes until the cheese starts to get a yellowish tint. Remove the cheese from the oven and evenly sift the paprika spice over the cheese, then place the cheese back in the oven for 2 more minutes, so that the spice infuses itself into the cheese.
4. Place a small frying pan on medium-high heat and add the chopped pistachios into the pan. Lightly roast the nuts for 2 minutes, then set aside.
5. Serve the cheese topped with the berry mixture, pistachio nuts. Slightly drizzle a little of the orange juice from the slices over the berry mix, then garnish the cheese with the leftover orange slices.

Nutrition: 584 Calories 4g Carbohydrates 46g Fat 33g Protein

132. Rhubarb Tart

Preparation Time: 10'

Servings: 8

Cooking Time: 45'

Ingredients

For the crust:
- 6 oz of almond flour
- 1/2 cup of erythritol
- ¾ oz of shredded coconut
- 3 oz of butter
- 1 tsp of cinnamon

For the filling:
- 4 ½ oz of butter
- ½ cup of erythritol
- 1 ¾ cups of almond flour
- 3 eggs
- 1 tsp of vanilla extract
- 7 oz of rhubarb
- 1 tsp of cinnamon
- ¼ cup of berries
- 2 tbsps. of sultanas (optional)

Directions

1. Preheat the oven to 360°F and prepare a tart dish of about 9" in size by lightly greasing it with a dollop of butter.
2. In a small, microwave safe bowl, add the 3 oz of butter into the bowl and place it in the microwave for a few seconds so that the butter melts. Set it aside to cool down.
3. In a medium bowl, pour in the almond flour, erythritol, coconut, and cinnamon. Mix the contents together until well combined.
4. Once the butter has cooled, pour it into the dry ingredient bowl whilst still stirring.
5. Spoon the dough mixture into the tart dish and use your hands to press the dough around the sides of the tart dish to form a pie crust. Press the dough firmly into the tart dish to ensure that there are no cracks and that the crust is as even as possible, then place it into the oven to bake for 10 minutes.
6. While the crust is baking, prepare the filling. Microwave the 4 ½ oz of butter in a microwave safe bowl for about 10 seconds so that the butter softens.
7. Pour the softened butter into a medium bowl, along with the erythritol, and beat the mixture until it's light and fluffy.
8. Pour the flour and vanilla into the bowl and crack the eggs into the mixture, while still beating the contents to mix the ingredients well. Cover the dish and set it aside.
9. In a separate bowl, use a vegetable peeler to cut long, thin strips of rhubarb and add the strips into the bowl. Add the 1 tsp of cinnamon, berries, and sultanas into the bowl and mix the contents together.
10. Remove the tart crust from the oven and spoon the flour filling into the crust, and even it out using a spoon. Then layer on the berry and rhubarb mixture.
11. Place the tart back into the oven for 35 more minutes.

Nutrition: 515 Calories 3g Carbohydrates 49g Fat 11g Protein

133. Saffron Panna Cotta

Preparation Time: 20' + 2H CHILLING TIME

Servings: 6

Cooking Time: 10'

Ingredients

- ½ tbsp of plain gelatin
- 2 cups of heavy cream
- ¼ tsp of vanilla extract
- 1 tbsp of honey
- a pinch of saffron
- a pinch of cinnamon
- 1 tbsp of chopped almonds
- 12 raspberries
- 1 slice of lemon
- ½ tsp of lemon rind

Directions

1. In a medium bowl, mix the gelatin with water (generally 1 tsp of gelatin needs 1 tbsp of water, but follow the instructions of your specific brand of gelatin, to make sure the mixture is correct). Mix well and set it aside.
2. Place a small saucepan over medium-high heat and add the cream, vanilla, saffron, and cinnamon into the pan. Mix the contents and bring to a light boil, then reduce the heat to a simmer for about 3 minutes so that the spices infuse well into the contents.
3. Remove the pan from the heat and pour the gelatin mixture into the pan, stirring it well to incorporate it.
4. Prepare 6 glasses/short serving bowls and evenly pour the mixture into the bowls. Sprinkle the lemon zest over the tops of the desserts, then cover the glasses with plastic wrap and place the desserts in the refrigerator for a minimum of 2 hours.
5. When the desserts are almost ready, place the almonds into a frying pan and lightly roast them for 3-5 minutes.
6. Sprinkle the almonds onto the panna cotta, then top each dessert with a few raspberries.
7. Lastly, squeeze the slice of lemon's juice over the desserts, and generously sprinkle the lemon zest over the top. Keep the dessert in the refrigerator until ready to serve.

Nutrition: 271 Calories 2g Carbohydrates 29g Fat 3g protein

Chapter 5

OLD AND MODERN PASTRY RECIPES

134. Chess Pie

Preparation Time: 6 H

Servings: 8

Cooking Time: 1 H

Ingredients

- 1 Pie crust
- 4 Eggs
- 1 ½ cup Granulated sugar
- ½ cup Butter - melted and cooled slightly
- ¼ cup Milk
- 1 tbsp White vinegar
- 2 tsp Pure vanilla extract
- ¼ cup Cornmeal
- 1 tbsp All-purpose flour
- ½ tsp Kosher salt

Directions

1. Warm the oven at 425° Fahrenheit. Roll out the pie crust and arrange it into the pie dish. Trim and crimp edges, and poke the center of the crust using a fork. Pop it into the freezer to chill for at least 15 minutes.
2. Arrange a layer of parchment baking paper inside the pie crust. Weigh it down using something such as dried beans to keep it flat. Bake until golden (15 min.). Carefully remove the parchment and pie weights and bake ten minutes more. Cool it while making the pie filling.
3. Adjust the oven temperature to 325° Fahrenheit. Whisk the eggs and sugar in a large mixing container. Melt and add the butter, milk, vinegar, and vanilla, whisking until incorporated. Mix in the cornmeal, flour, and salt until combined.
4. Dump the filling into the pie crust and bake until just set in the middle (50 min.). Cool the pie at room temperature for at least four hours. Then pop it into the fridge until ready to serve. Dust with powdered sugar before serving.

Nutrition: 43g carbs 14g fats 3g protein

135. Coconut Cream Pie Bars

Preparation Time: 40'

Servings: 15 VARIES

Cooking Time: 20'

Ingredients

Crust Ingredients:
- 1 cup Butter
- 2 cups A-P flour
- ½ cup Powdered sugar

Filling Ingredients:
- 3 cups Half-and-Half
- 4 Eggs
- 3 cups Coconut milk
- 1 ½ cup White sugar
- ½ tsp Salt
- 2/3 cup Cornstarch
- 1 ½ cup Flaked coconut
- ½ tsp Coconut extract
- ½ tsp Vanilla extract

Topping Ingredients:
- 2 cups Heavy whipping cream
- 1 tbsp cold Water
- 1 tsp Gelatin
- 3-4 tbsp Powdered sugar
- 1 cup Coconut - for toasting

Directions

1. Make the crust. Warm the oven at 350° Fahrenheit. Prepare the baking dish with a foil sling (if desired).
2. Combine the powdered sugar and flour. Dice and mix in the butter using a food processor (pulse it about 6-10 times) and press the mixture into the pan. Bake until light brown (18-20 min.) and cool it on a wire rack.
3. Toast the coconut. Spread one cup of the coconut flakes onto a baking tray and bake in the oven along with your shortbread crust for three to six minutes, stirring every minute or so until the coconut is golden brown. Spread it out on a plate to thoroughly cool.
4. Prepare the cream filling. Whisk the coconut milk, half-and-half, eggs, sugar, cornstarch, and salt in a large saucepan. Once boiling, adjust the temperature setting to med-low, whisking c until it's thick and bubbling (15-30 min.).
5. Add in the coconut and vanilla extracts and the 1.5 cups of untoasted coconut. Stir and dump the filling over the crust. Cool it on the countertop a short time and pop it into the refrigerator to chill about two to four hours until it's firm.
6. Prepare the topping. Measure and add one tablespoon cold water in a small bowl and sprinkle the gelatin evenly over the top. Let it soften for two minutes before microwaving it for 30 seconds and whisking to dissolve the gelatin.
7. Use a chilled bowl and beater to whisk two cups of heavy cream and powdered sugar until the cream forms stiff peaks. Stop and add the gelatin mixture about halfway through. Plop the cream over the bars and gently spread it around. Sprinkle on toasted coconut.
8. Pop it into the fridge to chill until serving time. Pull the bars out of the dish by slicing with a sharp knife to enjoy.

Nutrition: 40g carbs 12g fats 4g protein

136. Creamy Hazelnut Pie

Preparation Time: 10'

Servings: 8

Cooking Time: 40'

Ingredients

- 8 oz Room Temp cream cheese
- 1 cup Confectioner's sugar
- 1 ¼ cup Nutella - divided
- 8 oz Thawed - frozen whipped topping
- 9-inch crust Chocolate crumb

Directions

1. Cream the sugar, cream cheese, one cup of Nutella, and the confectioner's sugar. Fold in the topping and add the mixture to the crust. Warm the rest of the Nutella in a microwave for 15-20 seconds and drizzle it over the pie. Pop the pie into the fridge for at least four hours or overnight for the best results.

Nutrition: 47 carbs 15g fats 6g protein

137. The Famous Woolworth Ice Box Cheesecake

Preparation Time: 10'

Servings: 6

Cooking Time: 1 h

Ingredients

- 3 oz Lemon Jell-O
- 1 cup Boiling water
- 8 oz Cream cheese
- 1 cup Granulated sugar
- 5 tbsp Lemon juice
- 12 oz Evaporated milk - well chilled - ex. Carnation
- Graham crackers - crushed

Directions

1. Dissolve Jell-O in boiling water. Cool slightly until it's thickened. Combine the cream cheese, sugar, and lemon juice with an electric mixer until smooth. Add in the thickened Jell-O and mix. In another container, beat the milk until fluffy. Add the cream cheese mixture and blend well using the mixer. Line the baking tray with crushed crackers. Dump the filling into the pan and top with more crushed crackers and chill.

Nutrition: 40g carbs 10g fats 5g protein

138. Frozen Banana Split Pie

Preparation Time: 25'

Servings: 8

Cooking Time: 50'

Ingredients

- 3 tbsp Hard-shell ice cream topping - chocolate
- 9-inch Graham cracker crust
- 2 Bananas
- ½ tsp Lemon juice
- ½ cup Pineapple ice cream topping
- 1 quart Softened strawberry ice cream
- 2 cups Whipped topping
- ½ cup Toasted walnuts
- Chocolate syrup
- 8 Maraschino cherries with stems

Directions

1. Pour the chocolate topping into the crust and pop it into the freezer until chocolate is solid (5 min.). Slice and arrange the bananas in a bowl to toss with the juice. Place the bananas over the chocolate topping and layer using the pineapples, ice cream, whipped topping, and chopped nuts. Use a layer of plastic to cover the pie and freeze it until firm. Transfer it to the countertop to thaw for about 15 minutes before slicing it to serve. Top it off using the chocolate syrup and stemmed cherries.

Nutrition: 38g carbs 12g fats 6g protein

139. Frozen Peach Pie

| Preparation Time: | 30' | Servings: | 2 |

| Cooking Time: | 1 H |

Ingredients

- 2 ½ cups Graham cracker crumbs
- ½ cup and 2 tbsp Melted butter - divided
- ¼ cup Sugar
- 14 oz Sweetened condensed milk
- ¼ cup Orange juice
- ¼ cup Lemon juice
- 16 oz Frozen unsweetened sliced peaches
- 1 tbsp Grated lemon zest
- 1 ½ cups Heavy whipping cream
- Optional: Sweetened whipped cream (as desired)

Directions

1. Warm the oven at 350° Fahrenheit. Crumble and combine the cracker crumbs, sugar, and butter onto the bottom and up the sides of the two pie plates. Bake the pies until lightly browned (10-12 min.). Cool on wire racks.
2. Measure and add the milk, lemon juice, orange juice, peaches, and lemon zest into a blender and mix until smooth. Dump it into a mixing container. In another container, beat the cream until stiff peaks form and fold it into the peach mixture.
3. Scoop the filling into the crusts. Cover and freeze for at least four hours or until firm. Transfer the delicious pie to the table about 15 minutes before serving and top with whipped cream if desired.

Nutrition: 47g carbs 13g fats 9g protein

140. Key Lime Pie

Preparation Time: 20'

Servings: 8

Cooking Time: 45'

Ingredients

- ¼ cup Boiling water
- 0.3 oz Sugar-free lime gelatin
- 2 (6 oz) Key lime yogurt
- 6 oz Reduced-fat graham cracker crust
- 8 oz Frozen fat-free whipped topping

Directions

1. Boil the water and add it to the gelatin. Stir for about two minutes until it's dissolved. Whisk in the yogurt and topping. Pour it into the crust and pop in the fridge. Chill the pie for at least two hours and serve.

Nutrition: 45g carbs 13g fats 8g protein

141. Strawberry Lemonade Freezer Pie

Preparation Time: 15'

Servings: 8

Cooking Time: 50'

Ingredients

- 2 ½ cups Frozen & thawed - sliced sweet strawberries
- 3.4 oz Instant lemon pudding mix
- 8 oz Frozen - thawed whipped topping
- 9-inch Graham cracker crust
- Optional: Additional fresh berries & whipped topping

Directions

1. Combine the strawberries (with juices) and pudding mix in a large mixing container. Wait for about five minutes and fold in the whipped topping. Spread the filling into the crust. Freeze the pie for at least eight hours to overnight. Let it stand for five to ten minutes before serving.

Nutrition: 40g carbs 16g fats 7g protein

142. Sweet Potato Pie

Preparation Time:	2H

Servings:	8

Cooking Time:	1H

Ingredients

- 1 ¼ cup A-P flour
- 4 tbsp Leaf lard
- 4 tbsp Good-quality butter
- ¼ tsp Kosher salt
- 3-4 tbsp Ice water

The Potato Filling:
- 2 large Orange-fleshed California sweet potatoes
- ½ cup White sugar
- 2 lightly whisk Large eggs
- ¼ cup Half & Half - heavy cream
- ¾ tsp Cinnamon
- ¼ tsp Nutmeg - freshly grated
- ½ cup Light brown sugar
- 7 tbsp Unsalted butter
- Kosher salt

Directions

1. Cut the butter and lard into small pieces. Mix each of the dough components (omit the water) in a large mixing container. Knead the mixture until crumbly with a few lumps in it. Drizzle the mixture using the ice water and work the dough.
2. Shape the dough and wrap it in plastic wrap to chill it for one hour. When cold, scoop the dough onto a well-floured surface. Dust flour over the top. Knead the dough, adding flour as needed. Work the dough until it extends over the edges of the pie pan.
3. Warm the oven at 400° Fahrenheit. 'Blind-bake' the pie dough for 15 minutes.
4. Thoroughly cool it in the pan on a rack for about half an hour. Lower the oven temperature to 350° Fahrenheit.
5. Make the filling. Warm a pot of water using the high-temperature setting. Peel and slice the potatoes into one-inch cubes. Lower the setting to medium and toss in the potatoes to cook until (20 to 25 min.). Drain and rinse using cold water.
6. Toss them into a food processor to create a creamy purée. Measure and return 2.5 cups into the food processor. Whisk and add the eggs, butter, granulated sugar, half-and-half, nutmeg, cinnamon, and brown sugar. Mix until smooth and dump into the pie shell, smoothing the top.
7. Place the pie pan on a baking sheet and set a timer to bake until the crust is lightly golden and filling is almost set with a slight jiggle in the center (1 hr.).
8. Cool thoroughly on a wire rack. Place a layer of foil over the pie and pop in the fridge until it's time to serve.

Nutrition: 45g carbs 17g fats 7g protein

143. Blueberry Sour Cream Pound Cake

Preparation Time: 35'

Servings: 12

Cooking Time: 1 H

Ingredients

- 3 cups and 2 tbsp A-P flour - divided
- ½ tsp Baking soda
- 3 cups Sugar
- ½ tsp Salt
- 1 cup room temp - unsalted butter
- 1 cup Sour cream
- 6 Eggs
- 1 tsp Vanilla
- 2 cups Blueberries
- To Dust: Powdered sugar

Directions

1. Set the oven temperature setting at 325° Fahrenheit. Butter and flour a Bundt pan. Sift/whisk three cups of flour, salt, and baking soda to remove lumps. Set it to the side for now.
2. Mix the sugar and butter using an electric mixer until it is creamy. Add in sour cream and beat until it's combined. Alternate adding flour mixture and eggs, beating until just combined. Quickly mix in the vanilla.
3. Gently toss the blueberries and two tablespoons flour. Fold the blueberries into the batter. Dump the batter into the prepared pan and bake until golden and a toothpick inserted into the center comes out clean (1 ¼ hr.).
4. Cool it in the Bundt pan for at least ten minutes before turning onto a wire rack to cool completely. Once cool, dust it using a bit of powdered sugar.

Nutrition: 40g carbs 10g fat 5g protein

144 Carrot Cake Delight

Preparation Time: 25'

Servings: 2 (-INCH ROUNDS)

Cooking Time: 2 H

Ingredients

- 6 cups Grated carrots
- 1 cup Raisins
- 1 cup Brown sugar
- 4 Eggs
- 1 ½ cup White sugar
- 1 cup Vegetable oil
- 2 tsp Vanilla extract
- 1 cup Drained crushed pineapple
- 1 tsp Salt
- 3 cups A-P flour
- 1 ½ tsp Baking soda
- 4 tsp Ground cinnamon
- 1 cup Chopped walnuts

Directions

1. Grate the carrots and mix with the brown sugar. Set aside for about one hour and stir in the raisins. Warm the oven at 350° Fahrenheit. Grease and flour the cake pans. Whisk the eggs until light and mix in the white sugar, vanilla, and oil. Fold in the pineapple.
2. Sift or whisk the flour, cinnamon, baking soda, and salt, and fold into the wet mixture until absorbed. Lastly, fold in the carrot mixture and nuts. Pour into the prepared pans.
3. Bake for 45 to 50 minutes until the cake tests are completed using a toothpick. (Stick the center of the cakes; when done, it's clean. Transfer the pans to the countertop to cool for ten minutes before removing from the pan.
4. Wait for them to cool to frost with frosting and serve.

Nutrition: 41g carbs 13g fats 6g protein

145. Four Layer Pumpkin Cake with Frosting

Preparation Time: 30'

Cooking Time: 1 H

Servings: 16

Ingredients

- ½ tsp Fine sea salt
- 3 cups A-P flour
- 2 tsp Baking powder
- 1 tsp Chinese five-spice powder
- 1 tsp Baking soda
- 2 sticks room temp - unsalted butter
- 2 cups Golden brown sugar - packed
- 3 room temp eggs
- 15 oz Pure pumpkin
- 1/3 cup Whole milk

The Icing:
- 1 cup Unsalted – room temp butter
- 8 oz room temp cream cheese
- 1 tbsp Orange peel - finely grated
- 3 cups Powdered sugar - sifted
- ¼ cup Orange juice
- Walnut halves/chopped - toasted

Directions

1. Position the rack in the bottom third of the oven, warming it to reach 350° Fahrenheit. Spray the pans using a spritz of baking oil spray. Line the bottoms using a layer of parchment baking paper (lightly greasing the paper too).
2. Whisk the baking powder and soda, flour, salt, and 5-spice powder. Use an electric mixer to combine the butter and brown sugar in another large bowl until creamy. Mix in the eggs one at a time.
3. Fold in the pumpkin and dry fixings in three additions - alternately with milk in two additions. Dump the prepared batter into the baking trays.
4. Bake the cakes until the tester inserted into the center comes out clean (40 min.). Cool in pans on a rack for about 15 minutes. Loosen the edges with a small spatula and invert the cakes on cooling racks. Remove the parchment. Flip the cakes over onto racks and leave until thoroughly cooled.
5. Prepare the frosting using an electric mixer to mix the butter in a large mixing container until smooth. Mix in the cream cheese and orange peel, beating until creamy. Fold in and mix the powdered sugar (low speed).
6. Trim the rounded tops from cakes. Use a long-serrated knife to cut each cake horizontally in half. Arrange one cake layer, cut side up, onto a large platter. Spoon about 2/3 cup of frosting onto the cake - spreading to the edges.
7. Continue two more times with the cake and frosting. Top with the remaining cake layer with the cut side down. Decorate it using the rest of the frosting. Top it off using walnuts before serving.

Nutrition: 41g carbs 11g fats 5g protein

146. Georgia Peach Pound Cake

Preparation Time: 20'

Servings: 8

Cooking Time: 1 H

Ingredients

- 4 Eggs
- 1 cup Softened butter/margarine
- 3 cups A-P flour
- 2 cups White sugar
- ½ tsp Salt
- 1 tsp Baking powder
- 1 tsp Vanilla extract
- 2 cups Fresh peaches

Directions

1. Set the oven at 325°Fahrenheit. Butter a ten-inch tube pan and sprinkle with white sugar. Cream the sugar with the butter until it's fluffy. Whisk and fold in the eggs - one at a time - whisking after each addition. Mix in the vanilla.
2. Set aside ¼ of a cup of flour for later, and sift the rest of the flour with the baking powder and salt. Slowly mix it into the creamed mixture. Toss the reserved flour over the chopped peaches, and mix thoroughly into the batter. Dump the batter into the prepared pan.
3. Bake the cake for one hour and about 15 minutes. Leave the cake in the pan for about ten minutes, before placing it onto a wire rack to cool completely. For the sauce, puree a portion of the peaches, add two tablespoon cornstarch, and cook using the low-temperature setting until thickened. Serve the mixture as a sauce over the cake.

Nutrition: 45g carbs 12g fats 5g protein

147. Pineapple Pecan Cake with Frosting

Preparation Time: 40'

Servings: 8

Cooking Time: 15'

Ingredients

The Cake:
- 2 cups Sugar
- 2 tsp Baking soda
- 2 cups Flour
- 2 Eggs
- 20 oz Crushed pineapple with juice
- Optional: 1 cup Chopped pecans

The Icing:
- 1 stick Room Temp - softened butter
- 8 oz Cream cheese - softened
- 2 cups Confectioners' sugar
- 1 tbsp Vanilla

Directions

1. Whisk the sugar, flour, and baking soda in a large mixing container. Butter the baking pan and set the oven temperature setting at 350°Fahrenheit. Whisk and mix in the eggs, pineapple, and juice with the pecans. Mix just until moistened.
2. Dump the batter into the buttered pan. Set the timer to bake until done (30-35 min.). Transfer it to the countertop and wait for it to cool thoroughly. Prepare the icing by combining the butter, cream cheese, vanilla, and confectioners' sugar. Beat until smooth. Decorate the cake and serve.

Nutrition: 40g carbs 12g fats 4g protein

148. Red Velvet Cake

Preparation Time: 20'

Servings: 6 INCH CAKE

Cooking Time: 30'

Ingredients

The Cake:
- 1 ¼ cup A-P flour
- ¾ tsp Baking soda
- 1 tbsp Unsweetened cocoa powder
- ½ tsp Kosher salt
- ½ cup Coconut oil
- 1 cup Sugar
- 1 large Egg
- 1 tbsp Red food coloring
- ½ tsp Vinegar
- 1 ½ tsp Vanilla bean paste/extract
- ½ cup Buttermilk

The Frosting:
- ½ cup room temp - unsalted butter
- 4 oz room temp - cream cheese
- 2 cups Powdered sugar
- 1 tsp Vanilla bean paste or extract
- 1/8 tsp Kosher salt

Directions

1. Warm the oven to 350° Fahrenheit. Lightly grease the pans and set them aside for now. Whisk the salt, flour, baking soda, and cocoa powder. Prepare the mixer. Cream the coconut oil and sugar until fluffy (3-4 min.). Whisk and add the egg, food coloring, vanilla, and vinegar.
2. Mix in the dry components and buttermilk in two to three alternating additions and beat until just combined. Portion the batter between the cake pans and bake until a toothpick inserted into the center comes out clean (25 minutes).
3. Gently press down the top of the cakes to even them out while they're still hot. Cool them for ten minutes in their pans and turn them onto a wire rack to cool completely. Prepare the Frosting: Cream the butter and cream cheese in the stand mixer until combined. Add in the salt, powdered sugar, and vanilla.
4. To Assemble: Stack up the cooled cake layers with a thick layer of frosting in between. Frost and serve.
5. Note: For the oil, unrefined provides a hint of coconut flavor or use refined for no coconut flavor.

Nutrition: 45g carbs 13g fats 6g protein

149. Pumpkin Cheesecake

Preparation Time: 30' + 8H CHILLING TIME

Servings: 8-10

Cooking Time: 1 H 45'

Ingredients

- 2 ½ cups graham cracker crumbs
- ¾ cup unsalted butter, melted
- 2 ¾ cups granulated sugar, divided
- 1 teaspoon salt, plus a pinch
- 4 (8-ounce) blocks cream cheese, at room temperature
- ¼ cup sour cream
- 1 (15-ounce) can pure pumpkin
- 6 large eggs, room temperature
- 1 tablespoon vanilla extract
- 2 ½ teaspoons ground cinnamon
- 1 teaspoon ginger, ground
- ¼ teaspoon cloves, ground
- 2 cups whipped cream, sweetened
- 1/3 cup toasted pecans, roughly chopped

Directions

1. Preheat the oven to 325°F and grease a 12-inch springform pan.
2. In a mixing bowl, combine the graham cracker crumbs, melted butter, ¼ cup of the sugar, and a pinch of salt. Mix until well combined and press the mixture into the prepared springform pan. Bake for about 25 minutes.
3. While the crust is baking, begin making the filling by beating together the cream cheese, sour cream, and pumpkin.
4. Add the rest of the sugar, and slowly incorporate the beaten eggs and vanilla. Add the remaining salt, cinnamon, ginger, and cloves.
5. Fill a large baking pan (big enough to hold your springform pan) with about half an inch of water. Place it in the oven and let the water get hot.
6. Put foil around the edges of your springform pan, then add the filling and place the pan in the oven inside the water bath you made with the baking pan.
7. Bake for 1 hour and 45 minutes or until the center is set. You can turn the foil over the edges of the cake if it starts to get too brown. Remove the pan from the oven and place it on a cooling rack for at least one hour before removing the sides of the springform pan.
8. After it has cooled, remove sides of the pan and refrigerate the cheesecake for at least 8 hours or overnight. Serve with whipped cream and toasted pecans.

Nutrition: 45g carbs 12g fats 5g protein

150. Reese's Peanut Butter Chocolate Cake Cheesecake

Preparation Time: 2H + 6H CHILLING TIME

Servings: 8-10

Cooking Time: 1H 15'

Ingredients

Cheesecake
- 4 (8-ounce) packages cream cheese, softened
- 1 ¼ cups sugar
- ½ cup sour cream
- 2 teaspoons vanilla extract
- 5 eggs
- 8 Chocolate Peanut Butter cups, chopped
- 1 (14-ounce) can dulce de leche

Chocolate Cake
- 1 ¾ cups all-purpose flour
- 2 cups sugar
- ¾ cup cocoa
- 2 teaspoons baking soda
- 1 teaspoon salt
- 2 eggs, room temp
- 1 cup buttermilk
- ½ cup butter, melted
- 1 tablespoon vanilla extract
- 1 cup black coffee, hot

Peanut Butter Buttercream
- ¾ cup butter
- ¾ cup shortening
- ¾ cup peanut butter
- 1 ½ teaspoons vanilla
- 4-5 cups powdered sugar

Ganache
- 2 cups semi-sweet chocolate chips
- 1 cup heavy cream
- 1 teaspoon vanilla

Nutrition: 42g carbs 13g fats 5g protein

Directions

1. Preheat the oven to 350°F and grease a 9-inch springform pan. Make the cheesecake. Preheat the oven to 475°F. Fill a large baking pan (your springform pan with have to fit in it) with half an inch of water and place it in the oven while it preheats.
2. Beat the cream cheese in a large bowl until it is fluffy. Gradually incorporate the sugar, sour cream, and vanilla, and mix well.
3. Add the eggs one at a time and beat until just combined. Fold in the peanut butter cups and pour the batter into the springform pan. Bake at 475°F for 15 minutes, then reduce the heat to 350°F and bake for 60 minutes or until the center is completely set.
4. Remove the cake from the oven and let it cool for 60 minutes before taking off the sides of the springform pan. When it is completely cool, refrigerate the cheesecake for at least 6 hours, but 8 hours to overnight would be better. When it is completely cold, cut the cheesecake in half to make two layers.
5. Meanwhile, make the chocolate cake: mix the flour, sugar, cocoa, baking soda, and salt together in a large bowl. Mix in the eggs, buttermilk, melted butter, and vanilla, and beat until it is smooth. Slowly incorporate the coffee.
6. Grease and flour two 9-inch round cake pans. Pour the batter evenly into each pan and bake for 30–35 minutes. When fully cooked, remove the cakes from the oven and cool for 15 minutes before taking them out of the pans. When fully cooled, wrap each cake in plastic wrap and refrigerate until ready to assemble the cake.
7. Make the buttercream frosting by beating together the butter and shortening, then add the peanut butter and vanilla. Mix in the powdered sugar one cup at a time until you achieve the desired sweetness and consistency.
8. To assemble, put one layer of chocolate cake on a cake plate. Drizzle half of the dulce de leche over the top of the cake. Top that with a layer of cheesecake, and spread peanut butter frosting over the top of the cheesecake. Repeat to make a second layer. When assembled, place the whole cake in the freezer for about an hour to fully set.
9. Make the ganache by melting chocolate chips with heavy cream and vanilla in a small saucepan. When the cake is completely set, pour ganache over the top. Refrigerate until ganache the sets.

151. White Chocolate Raspberry Swirl Cheesecake

Preparation Time: 45' + 5H REFRIGERETION

Servings: 8-10

Cooking Time: 1H 45'

Ingredients

Crust
- 1 ½ cups chocolate cookie crumbs, such as crumbled Oreo® cookies
- 1/3 cup butter, melted

Filling
- 4 (8-ounce) packages cream cheese
- 1 ¼ cups granulated sugar
- ½ cup sour cream
- 2 teaspoons vanilla extract
- ½ cup raspberry preserves (or raspberry pie filling)
- ¼ cup water
- 5 eggs
- 4 ounces white chocolate, chopped into chunks

Optional Garnish
- 2 ounces shaved white chocolate (optional)
- Fresh whipped cream

Directions

1. Preheat the oven to 475°F. In a food processor, crumble the cookies and add the melted butter. Press the mixture into a greased 9-inch springform pan, and place in the freezer while you make the filling.
2. Pour half an inch of water in a large baking pan (it needs to fit your springform pan) and place it in the oven. In a mixing bowl, beat together the cream cheese, sugar, sour cream, and vanilla. Scrape the sides of the bowl after the ingredients have been well combined.
3. Beat the eggs in a small bowl, then add them slowly to the cream cheese mixture.
4. In another small dish, mix the raspberry preserves and water. Microwave for 1 minute. If you want to remove the raspberry seeds, you can run the hot liquid through a mesh strainer.
5. Remove the crust from the freezer and cover the outside bottom of the pan with aluminum foil. Sprinkle the white chocolate over the crust, then pour half of the cheesecake batter into the springform pan. Next, drizzle half of the raspberry preserves over the top of the batter. Then add the rest of the batter with the rest of the drizzle.
6. Place the springform pan into the water bath and bake for 15 minutes at 475°F, then reduce the heat to 350°F and bake about 60 more minutes more, or until the center of the cake is set and cake is cooked through.
7. Remove from oven and cool it completely before removing sides of the pan, then move to the refrigerator for at least 5 hours. Serve with extra white chocolate and fresh whipped cream.

Nutrition: 41g carbs 12g fats 4g protein

152. Carrot Cake Cheesecake

Preparation Time: 20' + 5H CHILLING TIME

Servings: 8

Cooking Time: 50-60'

Ingredients

Cheesecake
- 2 (8-ounce) blocks cream cheese, at room temperature
- ¾ cup granulated sugar
- 1 tablespoon flour
- 3 eggs
- 1 teaspoon vanilla

Carrot Cake
- ¾ cup vegetable oil
- 1 cup granulated sugar
- 2 eggs
- 1 teaspoon vanilla
- 1 cup flour
- 1 teaspoon baking soda
- 1 teaspoon cinnamon
- 1 dash salt
- 1 (8-ounce) can crushed pineapple, well-drained with juice reserved
- 1 cup grated carrot
- ½ cup flaked coconut
- ½ cup chopped walnuts

Pineapple Cream Cheese Frosting
- 2 ounces cream cheese, softened
- 1 tablespoon butter, softened
- 1 ¾ cups powdered sugar
- ½ teaspoon vanilla
- 1 tablespoon reserved pineapple juice

Nutrition: 40g carbs 11g fats 6g protein

Directions

1. Preheat the oven to 350°F and grease a 9-inch springform pan. In a large bowl, beat together the cream cheese and the sugar until smooth. Then beat in the flour, eggs, and vanilla until well combined. Set aside.
2. In another large bowl, beat together the ¾ cup vegetable oil, sugar, eggs, and vanilla until smooth. Then add the flour, baking soda, cinnamon, and salt and beat until smooth. Fold in the crushed pineapple, grated carrot, coconut, and walnuts.
3. Pour 1 ½ cups of the carrot cake batter into the prepared pan. Drop a large spoonful of the cream cheese batter over the top of the carrot cake batter. Then add a spoonful of carrot cake batter over the top of the cream cheese batter. Repeat with the remaining batter.
4. Bake the cake for 50–60 minutes, or until the center is set. Remove it from the oven and cool for about an hour before taking out the sides of the springform pan. Refrigerate for at least 5 hours.
5. While the cake is cooling, make the frosting. Beating together all the frosting ingredients. Frost the cake when it is completely cold.

153. Original Cheesecake

Preparation Time: 4 H 15'

Servings: 12

Cooking Time: 1 H 5'

Ingredients

- **Crust:**
- 1 ½ cups graham cracker crumbs
- ¼ teaspoon ground cinnamon
- 1/3 cup margarine, melted

Filling:
- 4 (8-ounce) packages cream cheese, softened
- 1 ¼ cups white sugar
- ½ cup sour cream
- 2 teaspoons vanilla extract
- 5 large eggs

Topping:
- ½ cup sour cream
- 2 teaspoons sugar

Directions

1. Preheat the oven to 475°F and place a skillet with half an inch of water inside. Combine the ingredients for the crust in a bowl. Line a large pie pan with parchment paper, and spread crust onto the pan. Press firmly. Cover it with foil, and keep it in the freezer until ready to use.
2. Combine all the ingredients for the filling EXCEPT the eggs in a bowl. Scrape the sides of the bowl while beating, until the mixture is smooth. Mix in eggs one at a time, and beat until fully blended.
3. Take the crust from the freezer and pour in the filling, spreading it evenly. Place the pie pan into the heated skillet in the oven, and bake for about 12 minutes.
4. Reduce the heat to 350°F. Continue to bake for about 50 minutes, or until the top of the cake is golden. Remove it from the oven and transfer the skillet onto a wire rack to cool.
5. Prepare the topping by mixing all ingredients in a bowl. Coat the cake with the topping, then cover. Refrigerate for at least 4 hours. Serve cold.

Nutrition: 41g carbs 11g fats 2g protein

154. Ultimate Red Velvet Cheesecake

Preparation Time: 3h 30'

Cooking Time: 1h 15'

Servings: 16

Ingredients

Cheesecake:
- 2 (8-ounce) packages cream cheese, softened
- 2/3 cup granulated white sugar
- Pinch salt
- 2 large eggs
- 1/3 cup sour cream
- 1/3 cup heavy whipping cream
- 1 teaspoon vanilla extract
- Non-stick cooking spray
- Hot water, for water bath

Red velvet cake:
- 2 ½ cups all-purpose flour
- 1 ½ cups granulated white sugar
- 3 tablespoons unsweetened cocoa powder
- 1 ½ teaspoons baking soda
- 1 teaspoon salt
- 2 large eggs
- 1 ½ cups vegetable oil
- 1 cup buttermilk
- ¼ cup red food coloring
- 2 teaspoons vanilla extract
- 2 teaspoons white vinegar

Frosting:
- 2 ½ cups powdered sugar, sifted
- 2 (8-ounce) packages cream cheese, softened
- ½ cup unsalted butter, softened
- 1 tablespoon vanilla extract

Nutrition: 39g carbs 12g fats 4g protein

Directions

1. For the cheesecake, preheat the oven to 325°F. Beat the cream cheese, sugar, and salt for about 2 minutes, until creamy and smooth. Add the eggs, mixing again after adding each one. Add the sour cream, heavy cream, and vanilla extract, and beat until smooth and well blended.
2. Coat a springform pan with non-stick cooking spray, then place parchment paper on top. Wrap the outsides entirely with two layers of aluminum foil. (This is to prevent water from the water bath from entering the pan.)
3. Pour the cream cheese batter into the pan, then place it in a roasting pan. Add boiling water to the roasting pan to surround the springform pan. Place it in the oven and bake for 45 minutes until set.
4. Transfer the springform pan with the cheesecake onto a rack to cool for about 1 hour. Refrigerate overnight.
5. For the red velvet cake, preheat the oven to 350°F. Combine the flour, sugar, cocoa powder, baking soda, and salt in a large bowl. In a separate bowl, mix the eggs, oil, buttermilk, food coloring, vanilla, and vinegar. Add the wet ingredients to dry ingredients. Blend for 1 minute with a mixer on medium-low speed, then on high speed for 2 minutes.
6. Spray non-stick cooking spray in 2 metal baking pans that are the same size as the springform pan used for the cheesecake. Coat the bottoms thinly with flour. Divide the batter between them.
7. Bake for about 30–35 minutes. The cake is made when only a few crumbs are attached to a toothpick when inserted in the center. Transfer the cakes to a rack and let them cool for 10 minutes. Separate the cakes from the pans using a knife around the edges, then invert them onto the rack. Let them cool completely.
8. To prepare the frosting, mix the powdered sugar, cream cheese, butter, and vanilla using a mixer on medium-high speed, just until smooth.
9. Assemble the cake by positioning one red velvet cake layer onto a cake plate. Remove the cheesecake from the pan, peel off the parchment paper, and layer it on top of the red velvet cake layer. Top with the second red velvet cake layer.
10. Coat a thin layer of prepared frosting on the entire outside of the cake. Clean the spatula every time you scoop out from the bowl of frosting, so as to not mix crumbs into it. Refrigerate for 30 minutes to set. Then coat the cake with a second layer by adding a large scoop on top, then spreading it to the top side of the cake then around it. Cut into slices. Serve.

155. Strawberry Shortcake

Preparation Time: 5'

Servings: 16

Cooking Time: 2h 15'

Ingredients

Sugared Strawberries:
- 2 cups strawberries (sliced)
- ¼ cup granulated sugar

Whipped Cream:
- 4 cups heavy cream
- ½ cup powdered sugar
- ¼ teaspoon vanilla

Shortcake Biscuit:
- 4 ½ cups all-purpose flour
- ½ cup sugar
- 5 tablespoons baking powder
- 2 teaspoons salt
- 1 ¾ cups butter
- 2 cups heavy cream
- 2 cups buttermilk
- 2 scoops vanilla ice cream

Directions

1. Preheat the oven to 375°F. In a bowl, combine the sliced strawberries with the sugar. Stir, cover, and refrigerate for 2 hours. Chill a mixing bowl and beat the heavy cream, powdered sugar, and vanilla until soft peaks form. Don't over beat or you will lose the fluffy consistency. Refrigerate.
2. In a mixing bowl, mix together the flour, sugar, baking powder, and salt. Stir to combine. Using two butter knives, cut the butter into the flour mixture until it becomes crumbly. Add the cream and the buttermilk and mix gently until the batter forms.
3. Turn out the dough onto a floured surface, and roll it to form biscuits about half an inch thick. Take care not to turn the cutter as you remove it from the dough. Place the biscuits on a non-stick cookie sheet and bake for about 15 minutes. They should at least double in size.
4. When they cool, assemble the shortcake by cutting each biscuit in half, topping the bottom half with strawberries and ice cream, and placing the top half of the biscuit on top of the ice cream. Top with more strawberries and whipped cream.

Nutrition: 40g carbs 12g fats 5g protein

156. Lemoncello Cream Torte

| Preparation Time: | 15' | | Servings: | 8-10 |

| Cooking Time: | 20' + 5H CHILLING TIME |

Ingredients

- 1 box yellow cake mix
- Limoncello liqueur (optional)
- 1 package ladyfinger cookies
- 1 (3-ounce) package sugar-free lemon gelatin
- 1 cup boiling water
- 1 (8-ounce) package cream cheese, softened
- 1 teaspoon vanilla extract
- 1 (13-ounce) can cold milnot (evaporated milk), whipped

For the glaze:
- 1 cup confectioner's sugar
- 1–2 tablespoons lemon juice

Directions

1. Preheat the oven to 350°F. Prepare the yellow cake mix according to the Directions on the package. Use two 9-inch round cake pans, or you can use a springform pan and cut the cake in half after it is baked.
2. When the cake is made and cooled, you can soak the layers lightly with some limoncello. Do the same with the ladyfingers. Bring one cup of water to a boil and stir in the lemon gelatin. Refrigerate until it gets thick, but don't let it set.
3. Mix together the cream cheese and vanilla, then mix in the thickened gelatin. Fold the whipped milnot into the mixture until combined. To assemble the cake, place the bottom layer of the cake back in the pan. This will help you get even layers. Top the cake with about half an inch of the lemon filling. Place ladyfingers on top of the filling, then top with another layer of the filling. Place the other half of the cake on the top.
4. Place the cake in the refrigerator to set. Make a drizzle with some lemon juice and confectioner's sugar, and drizzle over the cake.

Nutrition: 45g carbs 16g fats 5g protein

157. Oreo Cookie Cheesecake

| Preparation Time: | 10' + 4-6H CHILLING TIME | Servings: | 8-10 |

| Cooking Time: | 60' |

Ingredients

- 1 package Oreo cookies
- ☐ cup unsalted butter, melted
- 3 (8-ounce) packages cream cheese
- ¾ cup granulated sugar
- 4 eggs
- 1 cup sour cream
- 1 teaspoon vanilla extract
- Whipped cream and additional cookies for garnish

Directions

1. Preheat the oven to 350°F. Crush most of the cookies (25-30) in a food processor or blender, and add the melted butter. Press the cookie mixture into the bottom of a 9-inch springform pan and keep it in the refrigerator while you prepare the filling.
2. In a mixing bowl, beat the cream cheese until smooth, and add the sugar. Beat in the eggs in one a time. When the eggs are mixed together, beat in the sour cream and vanilla.
3. Chop the remaining cookies and fold them gently into the filling mixture. Pour the filling into the springform pan and bake at 350°F for 50–60 minutes. Ensure the center of the cake has set.
4. Let the cake cool for 15 minutes, then carefully remove the sides of the springform pan. Transfer to the refrigerator and refrigerate for 4–6 hours or overnight.

Nutrition: 47g carbs 18g fats 8g protein

158. Banana Cream Cheesecake

| Preparation Time: | 20' | Servings: | 4 |

| Cooking Time: | 1H 30' |

Ingredients

- 20 vanilla sandwich cookies
- ¼ cup margarine, melted
- 3 (8-ounce) packages cream cheese, softened
- 2/3 cup granulated sugar
- 2 tablespoons cornstarch
- 3 eggs
- ¾ cup mashed bananas
- ½ cup whipping cream
- 2 teaspoons vanilla extract

Directions

1. Preheat the oven to 350°F. Crush the cookies in either a food processor or blender. When they have turned to crumbs, add the melted butter. Place the mixture in a springform pan and press to entirely cover the bottom and up the sides of the pan. Refrigerate this while you prepare the filling.
2. Beat the cream cheese until it is smooth, and add the sugar and corn starch. When the cheese mixture is well blended, add in the eggs one at a time. When the eggs are incorporated, add the bananas, whipping cream, and vanilla, beating until well combined.
3. Pour the filling into the springform pan and bake at 350°F for 15 minutes. Reduce the heat to 200°F and bake until the center of the cheesecake is set, about 1 hour and 15 minutes.
4. When the center is set, remove the cake from the oven. Pop the spring on the pan, but don't remove the sides until the cheesecake has cooled completely. When it is cool, transfer it to the refrigerator. Refrigerate for at least 4 hours before serving. Serve with whipped cream and freshly sliced bananas.

Nutrition: 46g carbs 11g fats 5g protein

159. Blackout Cake

Preparation Time: 30'

Servings: 8-10

Cooking Time: 35-45'

Ingredients

For the Cake:
- 1 cup butter, softened
- 4 cups sugar
- 4 large eggs
- 4 teaspoons vanilla extract, divided
- 6 ounces unsweetened chocolate, melted
- 4 cups flour
- 4 teaspoons baking soda
- ½ teaspoon salt
- 1 cup buttermilk
- 1 ¾ cups boiling water

For the Chocolate Ganache:
- 12 ounces semisweet chocolate, chips or chopped
- 3 cups heavy cream
- 4 tablespoons butter, chopped
- 2 teaspoons vanilla
- 1 ½ cups roasted almonds, crushed (for garnish)

Directions

1. Preheat the oven to 350°F. Prepare two large rimmed baking sheets with parchment paper (or grease and dust with flour 3 8-inch cake pans).
2. In a large bowl or bowl for a stand mixer, beat together the butter and sugar until well combined. When the sugar mixture is fluffy, add the eggs and 2 teaspoons of vanilla. When that is combined, add the 4 ounces of melted chocolate and mix well.
3. In a separate bowl, stir together the flour, baking soda, and salt. Gradually add half the flour mixture to the chocolate mixture. When it is combined, add half of the buttermilk and mix until combined. Repeat with remaining flour mixture and buttermilk. When it is completely combined, add the boiling water and mix thoroughly. (The batter should be a little thin).
4. Divide the batter evenly between the two large baking sheets that you prepared earlier (or 3 8-inch cake pans).
5. Transfer to the oven and bake for 20–30 minutes for the baking sheets or 25-35 minutes for the cake pans, or until a toothpick inserted in the center comes out clean.
6. Remove from the oven and let cakes cool for about 10 minutes. With the pastry ring, make 3 cakes from each of the baking sheets. When they are completely cool down. If using cake pans, turn them out onto a cooling rack and let them cool completely and then cut horizontally into two to make 6 cake layers.
7. Make the ganache by mixing the chocolate chips and cream in a heat-safe glass bowl. Place the bowl over a pot of boiling water. Reduce heat to medium-low and let simmer gently. Stir constantly with a wooden spoon until the chocolate is all melted. Add-in the butter and vanilla and stir until well combined. Let cool for a few minutes, cover with plastic wrap, and refrigerate until the ganache holds its shape and is spreadable, about 10 minutes.
8. To assemble the cake, place the first cake layer on a serving plate and spread some of the ganache on the top. Place the second cake layer on top and spread some of the ganache on top. Repeat until all 6 layers are done. Use the remaining ganache to frost the top and sides of the cake, then cover the sides with crushed almonds (if desired) by pressing them gently into the chocolate ganache. Refrigerate before serving.

Nutrition: 41g carbs 10g fats 4g protein

160. Molten Lava Cake

Preparation Time: 20'

Servings: 5-6

Cooking Time: 10'

Ingredients

For the Cakes:
- Six tablespoons unsalted butter (2 tablespoons melted, four tablespoons at room temperature)
- 1/2 cup natural cocoa powder (not Dutch process), plus more for dusting
- 1 1/3 cups all-purpose flour
- One teaspoon baking soda
- 1/2 teaspoon baking powder
- 1/2 teaspoon salt
- Three tablespoons milk
- 1/4 cup vegetable oil
- 1 1/3 cups sugar
- 1 1/2 teaspoons vanilla extract
- Two large eggs, at room temperature

For the Fillings and Toppings:
- 8 ounces bittersweet chocolate, finely chopped
- 1/2 cup heavy cream
- Four tablespoons unsalted butter
- One tablespoon light corn syrup
- Caramel sauce, for drizzling
- 1-pint vanilla ice cream

Nutrition: 546 Calories 5g Protein 61g Carbohydrate 31g Fat

Directions

1. Oven preheats to 350 degrees F. Make the cakes: Brush four one 1/4-cup brioche molds (jumbo muffin cups or 10-ounce ramekins) with the butter melted in 2 tablespoons. Clean the cocoa powdered molds and tap the excess.
2. In a small bowl, whisk in the flour, baking soda, baking powder, and salt. Bring 3/4 cup water & the milk and over medium heat to a boil in a saucepan; set aside.
3. Use a stand mixer, combine vegetable oil, four tablespoons of room-temperature butter and sugar and beat with the paddle attachment until it's fluffy at medium-high speed, around 4 minutes, scrape the bowl down and beat as desired. Add 1/2 cup cocoa powder and vanilla; beat over medium velocity for 1 minute. Scrape the pot beneath. Add one egg and beat at medium-low speed for 1 minute, then add the remaining egg and beat for another minute.
4. Gradually beat in the flour mixture with the mixer on a low level, then the hot milk mixture. Finish combining the batter with a spatula of rubber before mixed. Divide the dough equally between the molds, each filling slightly more than three-quarters of the way.
5. Move the molds to a baking sheet and bake for 25 to 30 minutes, until the tops of the cakes feel domed, and the centers are just barely set. Move the baking sheet to a rack; allow the cakes to cool for about 30 minutes before they pull away from the molds.
6. How to set up the Cake: Make the Filling: Microwave the sugar, butter, chocolate, and corn syrup in a microwave-safe bowl at intervals of 30 seconds, stirring each time, until the chocolate starts to melt, 1 minute, 30 seconds. Let sit for three minutes and then whisk until smooth. Reheat, if possible, before use.
7. Using a paring knife tip to remove the cakes gently from the molds, then invert the cakes onto a cutting board.
8. Hollow out a spoon to the cake; save the scraps. Wrap the plastic wrap and microwave cakes until steaming, for 1 minute.
9. Drizzle the caramel plates, unwrap the cakes, then put them on top. Pour three tablespoons into each cake filling.
10. Plug in a cake scrap to the door. Save any leftover scraps or discard them.
11. Top each cake, use an ice cream scoop. Spoon more chocolate sauce on top, spread thinly so that it is coated in a jar.

161. White Chocolate Raspberry Nothing Bundt Cakes

| Preparation Time: | 20' | Servings: | 5-6 |

| Cooking Time: | 10' |

Ingredients

- Chopped into small cubes, 200g butter, plus extra for greasing
- 100g white chocolate, broken into pieces
- Four large eggs
- 200g caster sugar
- 200g self-rising flour
- 175g raspberries, fresh or frozen

For the ganache
- 200g white chocolate, chopped
- 250ml double cream
- A little icing sugar, for dusting

Directions

1. Heat oven to fan/gas 4, 180C/160C. Grease and line the 2 x 20 cm round base with loose-bottomed cake tins. In a heat-proof mixing bowl, place the butter and chocolate, set over a pan of barely simmering water, and allow to melt gradually, stirring occasionally.
2. Once butter and chocolate have melted, remove from heat and cool for 1-2 minutes, then beat with an electric whisk in the eggs and sugar. Fold and raspberries in the starch.
3. Pour the mixture gently into the tins and bake for 20-25 minutes or until golden brown and a skewer inserted in the center is clean (Don't be fooled by their juiciness, the raspberries leave a residue on the skewer). Pullout the cakes from the oven & allow for 10 minutes of cooling in the tins before placing on a wire rack.
4. To make the ganache, place the chocolate over a pan of barely simmering water in a heatproof bowl with 100ml of the cream on top. Remove until the chocolate has melted into the sugar, and leave a smooth, shiny ganache on you. You need to leave the ganache at room temperature to cool, then beat in the rest of the cream.
5. Sandwich them together with the chocolate ganache after the cakes have cooled. Just before serving, sprinkle them with icing sugar.

Nutrition: 489 Calories 3.9g Protein 59g Carbohydrate 28g Fat

162. Caramel Rockslide Brownies

Preparation Time: 25'

Servings: 5-6

Cooking Time: 25'

Ingredients

- 1 cup butter (2 sticks)
- 2 cups of sugar
- Four eggs
- Two teaspoons vanilla extract
- 2/3 cup unsweetened natural cocoa powder
- 1 cup all-purpose flour
- 1/2 teaspoon salt
- One teaspoon baking powder
- 1/2 cup semisweet chocolate chips
- 1 cup (plus more for drizzling over the top) caramel topping
- 3/4 cup chopped pecans (plus more for sprinkling on top)

Directions

1. Preheat to 350 degrees on the oven. On a medium saucepan, melt butter over medium heat.
2. Clear from heat the pan and whisk in sugar. Whisk in the vanilla extract & the eggs. Mix the cocoa, baking powder, flour, salt and in a separate dish. Drop the dry ingredients into the saucepan and combine them until they have just been added. Add chocolate chips.
3. Pour the batter into two nine by 9-inch baking pans that are evenly split, sprayed with nonstick spray, and lined with parchment paper.
4. Bake for 25-28 minutes and leave to cool.
5. Use the parchment paper edges to lift the whole brownie out of one of the pans, and chop into 1/2-inch cubes.
6. Pour 1 cup of caramel over the brownies still in the saucepan, then add the chopped pecans and brownie cubes.
7. Press down to make the caramel stick to the brownie cubes. If desired, drizzle with extra caramel and sprinkle with a few more chopped pecans.
8. If needed, serve with ice cream and excess sugar, and chopped pecans.

Nutrition: 509 Calories 5g Protein 67g Carbohydrate 32g Fat

163. Cornbread Muffins

Preparation Time: 10'

Servings: 6-7

Cooking Time: 25'

Ingredients

- ½ cup butter softened
- 2/3 Cup white sugar
- ¼ cup honey
- Two eggs
- ½ teaspoon salt
- 1 ½ cups all-purpose flour
- ¾ cup cornmeal
- ½ teaspoon baking powder
- ½ cup milk
- ¾ cup frozen corn kernels, thawed

Directions

1. Preheat oven to 400 grades F (200 grades C). Grease or 12 cups of muffins on deck.
2. Cream the butter, sugar, honey, eggs, and salt together in a big pot. Add in rice, cornmeal, and baking powder, blend well. Stir in corn and milk. Pour the yield into prepared muffin cups or spoon them.
3. Bake for 20 to 25 minutes in a preheated oven until a toothpick inserted in the center of a muffin comes out clean.

Nutrition: 141 Calories 6g Protein 22g Carbohydrate 18g Fat

164. Chocolate Mousse Cake

Preparation Time: 10'

Servings: 6-7

Cooking Time: 25'

Ingredients

- 1 (18.25 ounce) chocolate cake mix pack
- 1 (14 ounces) can sweeten condensed milk
- 2 (1 ounce) squares unsweetened chocolate, melted
- ½ cup of cold water
- 1 (3.9 ounces) package instant chocolate pudding mix
- 1 cup heavy cream, whipped

Directions

1. Preheat oven up to 175 degrees C (350 degrees F). Prepare and bake cake mix on two 9-inch layers according to package Directions. Cool off and pan clean.
2. Mix the sweetened condensed milk and melted chocolate together in a big tub. Stir in water slowly, then pudding instantly until smooth. Chill in for 30 minutes, at least.
3. Remove from the fridge the chocolate mixture, and whisk to loosen. Fold in the whipped cream and head back to the refrigerator for at least another hour.
4. Place one of the cake layers onto a serving platter. Top the mousse with 1 1/2 cups, then cover with the remaining cake layer. Frost with remaining mousse, and cool until served. Garnish with chocolate shavings or fresh fruit.

Nutrition: 324 Calories 8g Protein 32g Carbohydrate 50g Fat

165. Blackberry and Apples Cobbler

Preparation Time: 10'

Servings: 6

Cooking Time: 30'

Ingredients

- ¾ cup stevia
- 6 cups blackberries
- ¼ cup apples, cored and cubed
- ¼ teaspoon baking powder
- 1 tablespoon lime juice
- ½ cup almond flour
- ½ cup of water
- 3 and ½ tablespoon avocado oil
- Cooking spray

Directions

1. In a bowl, mix the berries with half of the stevia and lemon juice, sprinkle some flour all over, whisk and pour into a baking dish greased with cooking spray.
2. In another bowl, mix flour with the rest of the sugar, baking powder, the water, and the oil, and stir the whole thing with your hands.
3. Spread over the berries, introduce in the oven at 375° F, and bake for 30 minutes. Serve warm.

Nutrition: 221 Calories 6.3g Fat 3.3g Fiber 6g Carbohydrates 9g Protein

166. Black Tea Cake

Preparation Time: 10'

Servings: 8

Cooking Time: 35'

Ingredients

- 6 tablespoons black tea powder
- 2 cups almond milk, warmed up
- 1 cup avocado oil
- 2 cups stevia
- 4 eggs
- 2 teaspoons vanilla extract
- 3 and ½ cups almond flour
- 1 teaspoon baking soda
- 3 teaspoons baking powder

Directions

1. In a bowl, combine the almond milk with the oil, stevia, and the rest of the ingredients and whisk well.
2. Pour this into a cake pan lined with parchment paper, introduce in the oven at 350° F and bake for 35 minutes. Leave the cake to cool down, slice, and serve.

Nutrition: 200 Calories 6.4g Fat 4g Fiber 6.5g Carbohydrates 5.4g Protein

167. Quinoa Muffins

Preparation Time: 10'

Cooking Time: 30'

Servings: 12

Ingredients

- 1 cup quinoa, cooked
- 6 eggs, whisked
- Salt and black pepper to the taste
- 1 cup Swiss cheese, grated
- 1 small yellow onion, chopped
- 1 cup white mushrooms, sliced
- ½ cup sun-dried tomatoes, chopped

Directions

1. In a bowl, combine the eggs with salt, pepper, and the rest of the ingredients and whisk well.
2. Divide this into a silicone muffin pan, bake at 350 degrees F for 30 minutes and serve for breakfast.

Nutrition: 123 Calories 5.6g Fat 1.3g Fiber 10.8g Carbohydrates 7.5g Protein

168. Figs Pie

Preparation Time: 10'

Cooking Time: 1 H

Servings: 8

Ingredients

- ½ cup stevia
- 6 figs, cut into quarters
- ½ teaspoon vanilla extract
- 1 cup almond flour
- 4 eggs, whisked

Directions

1. Spread the figs on the bottom of a springform pan lined with parchment paper.
2. In a bowl, combine the other ingredients, whisk and pour over the figs,
3. Bake at 375° F for 1 hour, flip the pie upside down when it's done and serve.

Nutrition: 200 Calories 4.4g Fat 3g Fiber 7.6g Carbohydrates 8g Protein

Chapter 6

Soft Drink Recipes

169. Lemon and Berry Slush

Preparation Time: 5'

Servings: 7

Cooking Time: 0'

Ingredients

- 1 cup soda, lemon and lime flavored
- 2 cups strawberries, cut into half
- 1/3 cup lemon juice
- 1/4 cup sugar
- 3 cups of ice cubes

Directions

1. Put all the ingredients and fill it to the max water line, then blend until smooth. Plug in a food processor, place all the ingredients in the order as mentioned in the ingredients list and then pulse for 1 to 2 minutes until frothy.
2. Divide the slush evenly between four glasses and then serve.

Nutrition: 110 Calories 29.7 g Carbohydrates 0.25 g Fiber 29 g Sugars

170. Taco Bell's Pena Colada Drink

Preparation Time: 5'

Cooking Time: 0'

Servings: 4

Ingredients

- ½ cup lemon and lime soda pop
- 1 cup Pina colada mix
- 1 cup crushed ice
- 2 slices of lime

Directions

1. Plug in a food processor, place all the ingredients in it except for lime slices and then pulse for 1 to 2 minutes until frothy.
2. Divide the drink evenly between two glasses, top with lime slices, and then serve.

Nutrition: 245 Calories 2.7g Fat 32g Carbohydrates 0.4g Fiber 21.5g Sugars

171. Chick fil-A Lemonade

Preparation Time: 5'

Servings: 4

Cooking Time: 0'

Ingredients

- 1 ¾ cup lemon juice
- 5 cups water, cold
- 1 cup of sugar

Directions

1. Take a large jug or a pitcher, pour in lemon juice, and then stir in sugar until dissolved.
2. Pour in water, stir until mixed, and then chill it in the refrigerator for a minimum of 1 hour before serving.

Nutrition: 217 Calories 1 g Fat 57 g Carbohydrates 1 g Fiber 53 g Sugars 1 g Protein

172. Dairy Queen Blizzard

Preparation Time: 5'

Servings: 2

Cooking Time: 0'

Ingredients

- 8 Oreo Double Stuff cookies
- 4 cups vanilla ice cream
- 8 mini Oreo cookies

Directions

1. Take a large bowl, place ice cream in it, and then beat it until creamy.
2. Break Oreo cookies into chunks, add to the ice cream and then fold by using a spoon until mixed.
3. Divide evenly between two glasses, top with mini Oreo cookies, and then serve.

Nutrition: 580 Calories 24 g Fat 80 g Carbohydrates 1 g Fiber 67 g Sugars 15 g Protein

173. Watermelon and Mint Lemonade

| **Preparation Time:** 5' | **Servings:** 6 |

Cooking Time: 0'

Ingredients

- ½ cup chopped mint leaves
- 4 cups water, chilled
- 1 cup of sugar
- 2 cups watermelon juice
- 1 ½ cups lemon juice

Directions

1. Take a large jug or a pitcher, pour in lemon juice, stir in sugar until dissolved, and then stir in mint leaves.
2. Pour in the water, stir until mixed, and then stir in watermelon juice.
3. Let the lemonade chill for 1 hour in the refrigerator and then serve.

Nutrition: 220 Calories 55 g Carbohydrates 12 g Fiber 53 g Sugars

174. Sonic Ocean Water

Preparation Time: 5'

Servings: 2

Cooking Time: 0'

Ingredients

- 2 limes, juiced
- 1 teaspoon coconut extract, unsweetened
- 1 tablespoon sugar
- 2 tablespoons water
- 1 teaspoon blue food coloring
- 2 bottles of Sprite, each about 12 ounces
- ½ cup crushed ice

Directions

1. Take a small bowl, place it water, stir in sugar until dissolved, and then let it cool until chilled.
2. Fill two glasses evenly with crushed ice and then pour in the sprite.
3. Add coconut extract into the chilled sugar mixture, stir until mixed, and then stir in food color.
4. Add the coconut extract mixture evenly into each glass, stir until mixed, and then serve.

Nutrition: 116 Calories 30.2 g Carbohydrates 30.2 g Sugars

175. Rainforest Café's Strawberry Lemonade

Preparation Time: 5'

Servings: 8

Cooking Time: 5'

Ingredients

- ¾ cup of sugar
- 1-pound strawberries, fresh, diced
- 6 cups water, chilled
- 1 lemon, zested
- 6 lemons, juiced

Directions

1. Take a small saucepan, place it over medium-high heat, and then add berries in it. Pour in 1 cup water, stir in lemon zest and then bring the mixture to a boil.
2. Transfer strawberry mixture into a pitcher, add remaining water along with lemon juice and then stir until combined. Taste to adjust sweetener if needed and then let it chill for 1 hour in the refrigerator before serving.

Nutrition: 487 Calories 132 g Carbohydrates 5 g Fiber 122 g Sugars

176. Chick-fil-A's Frozen Lemonade Copycat

Preparation Time: 10'

Servings: 3

Cooking Time: 0'

Ingredients

- 1/2 c. freshly squeezed lemon juice
- 1/2 c. sugar
- 2 c. water
- 6 c. vanilla ice cream
- sliced lemons, for garnish

Directions

1. Dissolve the sugar in lemon juice. Add water and chill to dilute.
2. Stir lemonade and ice cream into a blender. Mix until smooth, and split between 3 cups. Garnish with lemon slices, and serve.

Nutrition: 470 calories 3g fiber 120g sugar

177. Dunkin Donut's Mint Hot Chocolate Copycat

| Preparation Time: | 5' | Servings: | 53 |

| Cooking Time: | 0' |

Ingredients

- 7-1/2 cups instant chocolate drink mix
- 1 package (25.6 ounces) nonfat dry milk powder
- 2-1/2 cups confectioners' sugar
- 1 cup powdered nondairy creamer
- 25 peppermint candies, crushed
- Miniature marshmallows

Each Servings:
- 1 cup hot whole milk

Directions

1. Combine the initial 5 ingredients. Divide into gift bags, or growing them in an airtight tub, adding as desired miniature marshmallows. Mixing can take up to 6 months to store in a cold, dry location.
2. To make hot cocoa: place 1/3 cup cocoa mix in a mug. Incorporate hot milk until blended. Fill in as many marshmallows as you wish.

Nutrition: 420 calories 3g fiber 112g sugar

178. Tim Horton's Hot Apple Cider Copycat

Preparation Time: 2H 5'

Servings: About 2 quarts

Cooking Time: 0'

Ingredients

- 8 whole cloves
- 4 cups apple cider or juice
- 4 cups pineapple juice
- 1/2 cup water
- 1 cinnamon stick (3 inches)
- 1 teabag

Directions

1. Place the cloves on a double cheesecloth thickness; bring up cloth corners and tie to form a bag with kitchen string. Place the rest of the ingredients into 3-qt. Slow cooker; add a bag of spices.
2. Cover and cook for 2 hours on medium, or until the ideal temperature hits cider. Until serving, remove the spice packet, cinnamon stick, and teacup.

Nutrition: 401 calories 6g fiber 110g sugar

179. New Orleans' Famous Hurricanes Copycat

Preparation Time: 10'

Servings: 6

Cooking Time: 0'

Ingredients

- 2 cups passion fruit juice
- 1 cup plus 2 tablespoons sugar
- 3/4 cup lime juice
- 3/4 cup light rum
- 3/4 cup dark rum
- 3 tablespoons grenadine syrup
- 6 to 8 cups ice cubes
- Orange slices, starfruit slices, and maraschino cherries

Directions

1. Combine the fruit juice, sugar, lime juice, rum, and grenadine into a pitcher; whisk until sugar is dissolved.
2. Pour into ice-cold glasses filled with hurricane or highball. Serve with slices of orange, starfruit, and cherries.

Nutrition: 403 calories 3.8g fiber 103g sugar

180. Ruby Tuesday's Raspberry Iced Tea Copycat

Preparation Time: 25'

Servings: 15

Cooking Time: 0'

Ingredients

- 4 quarts water
- 10 tea bags
- 1 (12 ounces) frozen unsweetened raspberries
- 1 cup sugar
- 3 tbsp lime juice

Directions

1. Let the 2 quarts of water boil in a saucepan; remove from heat. Add tea bags; steep, sealed, on taste for 5-8 minutes. Discard the bags for tea.
2. In a large saucepan, put the raspberries, sugar, and remaining water; bring to a boil, stirring to dissolve sugar. Reduce heat; simmer for 3 minutes, uncovered. Push the mixture into a bowl through a fine-mesh strainer; discard the pulp and seeds.
3. Combine the tea, raspberry syrup, and lime juice into a large pitcher. Cover, refrigerate, until cold.

Nutrition: 120 calories 4g fiber 104g sugar

181. Mike's Hard Lemonade Copycat

Preparation Time: 5'

Servings: 2

Cooking Time: 0'

Ingredients

- 2-1/4 cups sugar
- 5 cups water, divided
- 1 tablespoon grated lemon zest
- 1-3/4 cups lemon juice
- 1 cup light rum or vodka
- 6 to 8 cups ice cubes

Garnish:
- Lemon slices

Directions

1. Combine the sugar, 1 cup of water, and lemon zest into a large saucepan. Cook over medium heat and stir until sugar dissolves, about 4 minutes. Out of heat strip. Stir in the juice of the lemon and the remaining vapor. Offer in a 2-qt. Pitcher; leave to cool until chilled.
2. Stir the rum in. Place 3/4 to 1 cup of ice in a highball glass for each serving. Pour lemonade into the glass. Garnish as desired, with lemon slices.

Nutrition: 402 calories 4.9g fiber 104.3g sugar

182. Chick-fil-A's Frosted Lemonade Copycat

Preparation Time: 10'

Servings: 4

Cooking Time: 0'

Ingredients

- 2 tbsp lemon drop candies
- 1 tsp sugar
- 1/2 small lemon
- 1/2 cup milk
- 2 cups vanilla ice cream
- 2 cups lemon sorbet
- 3 ounces cream cheese
- 2 tsp lemon zest
- 1/2 tsp vanilla extract

Directions

1. Mix the crushed lemon drops and the sugar in a shallow dish. Moisten the rims of four glasses using 1 or 2 lemon slices; dip the edges into a candy mixture.
2. Place the remaining ingredients in a blender (minus lemon slices); cover and process until smooth. Pour into prepared glasses; immediately serve with remaining slices of lemon.

Nutrition: 411 calories 6g fiber 112g sugar

183. Crystal Light's Berry Sangria Mix Copycat

Preparation Time: 15'

Servings: 10

Cooking Time: 0'

Ingredients

- 1 bottle (750 ml) sparkling white wine
- 2-1/2 cups white cranberry juice
- 2/3 cup light or coconut rum
- 1/3 cup each fresh blackberries, blueberries, and raspberries
- 1/3 cup chopped fresh strawberries
- Ice cubes

Directions

1. Mix wine, juice, and rum in a large saucepan; add fruit. Refrigerate to a total of 2 hours; serve over ice.

Nutrition: 403 calories 4.9g fiber 117g sugar

Chapter 7

Practical Advice for Beginners to Canning and Preserving your Favorite Foods

There are a few safety tips that you should follow when you start canning and preserving foods from home. Canning is a great way to store and preserve foods, but it can be risky if not done correctly. However, if you follow these tips, you will be able to can foods safely.

Choose the Right Canner

The first step to safe home canning is choosing the right canner. First off, know when to use a pressure canner or a water bath canner.

Use a pressure canner that is specifically designed for canning and preserving foods. There are several types of canner out there, and some are just for cooking food, not for preserving food and processing jars. Be sure that you have the right type of equipment.

Make sure your pressure canner is the right size. If your canner is too small, the jars may be undercooked. Always opt for a larger canner as the pressure on the bigger pots tends to be more accurate, and you will be able to take advantage of the larger size and can more foods at once!

Before you begin canning, check that your pressure canner is in good condition. If your canner has a rubber gasket, it should be flexible and soft. If the rubber is dry or cracked, it should be replaced before you start canning. Be sure your canner is clean, and the small vents in the lid are free of debris. Adjust your canner for high altitude processing if needed.

Once you are sure your canner is ready to go and meets all these guidelines, it is time to start canning!

Opt for a Screw Top Lid System

There are many kinds of canning jars that you can choose to purchase. However, the only type of jar approved by the USDA is a mason jar with a screw-top lid. These are designated "preserving jars" and are considered the safest and most effective option for home preserving uses.

Some jars are not thought to be safe for home preservation despite being marketed as canning jars. Bail Jars, for example, have a two-part wire clasp lid with a rubber ring in between the lid and jar. While these were popular in the past, it is now thought that the thick rubber and tightly closed lid does not provide a sufficient seal, leading to a higher potential for botulism. Lightening Jars should not be used for canning as they are simply glass jars with glass lids, with no rubber at all. That will not create a good seal!

Reusing jars from store-bought products is another poor idea. They may look like they're in good condition, but they are typically designed to be processed in a commercial facility. Most store-bought products do not have the two-part band and lid system, which is best for home canning. The rubber seal on a store-bought product is likely not reusable once you open the original jar. You can reuse store-bought jars at home for storage but not for canning and preserving.

Check Your Jars, Lids, and Bands

As you wash your jars with soapy water, check for any imperfections. Even new jars may have a small chip or crack and need to be discarded. You can reuse jars again and again as long as they are in good condition.

The metal jar rings are also reusable; however, you should only reuse them if they are rust free and undented. If your bands begin to show signs of wear, consider investing in some new ones.

Jar lids need to be new as the sealing compound on the lid can disintegrate over time. When you store your jars in damp places (like in a basement or canning cellar), the lids are even more likely to disintegrate. Always use new lids to ensure that your canning is successful.

Check for Recent Canning Updates

Canning equipment has changed over the years, becoming higher-tech and, therefore, more efficient at processing foods. In addition to the equipment becoming more advanced, there have also been many scientific improvements, making canning safer when the proper steps are taken. For example, many people used to sterilize their jars before pressure canning. While this is still okay to do, it is unnecessary as science has shown that any bacteria in the jars will die when heated to such a high temperature in a pressure canner. Sterilization is an extra step that you don't need!

Make sure that your food preservation information is all up to date and uses current canning guidelines. Avoid outdated cookbooks and reassess "trusted family methods" to make sure they fit into the most recent criteria for safe canning. When in doubt, check with the US Department of Agriculture's Complete Guide to Home Canning, which contains the most recent, up-to-date canning tips.

Pick the Best Ingredients

When choosing food to can, always get the best food possible. You want to use high quality, perfectly ripe produce for canning. You will never end up with a jar of food better than the product itself, so picking good ingredients is important to your final product's taste. Also, products that past their prime can affect the ability to handle it. If strawberries are overripe, your jam may come out too runny. If your tomatoes are past their prime, they may not have a high enough pH level to be processed in a water bath. Pick your ingredients well, and you will make successfully preserved foods.

Clean everything

While you may know that your jars and lids need to be washed and sanitized, don't forget about the rest of your tools. Cleaning out your canner before using it is essential, even if you put it away clean. Make sure to wipe your countertop well, making sure there are no crumbs or residue. Wash your produce with clean, cold water, and don't forget to wash your hands! The cleaner everything is, the less likely you are to spread bacteria onto your jarred foods.

Follow Your Recipe

Use recipes from trusted sources, and be sure to follow them to the letter. Changing the amount of one or two ingredients may alter the balance of acidity and result in unsafe canning (especially when using a water bath canner). Use the ingredients as directed and make very few changes—none if possible.
Adhere to the processing times specified by your recipe. Sometimes the times may seem a little long, but the long processing time makes these products safe to store on the shelf. The processing time is the correct amount of time needed to destroy spoilage organisms, mold spores, yeast, and pathogens in the jar. So, as you may have guessed, it is extremely important to use the times written in your recipe as a hard rule.

Cool the Jars

Be sure that you give your jars 12 hours to cool before testing the seal. If you test the seal too early, it may break as the jar is still warm, making it pliable. Be sure to cool the jars away from a window or fan as even a slight breeze may cause the hot jars to crack. Once cool, remove the metal band, clean it and save it for your next canning project.

Conclusion

Creativity often happens when you cook at home, and you can attach a range of plant foods to a variety of colors. You are not only acquiring kilograms, antioxidants, minerals, and phytonutrients but also introducing nice textures and colors to your meals. You would be shocked by how much food in a single dish is collected.

Portion control from home can be regulated. When food is cooked for us, we tend to eat all or most of it. Try to use little dishes at home, but ensure that all good things like vegetables, fruits, whole grains, and legumes are filled. You are certainly going to be satisfied and happy.

The major advantage of trying copycat restaurant recipes is that you can save more money and use your creativity to improve the dish. You can also adjust the ingredients and add those favorite herbs to your desired taste. Now you have saved your money and restaurant-quality dishes for your family as well.

You may not include some ingredients of your favorite dish when you try the copycat recipes, and it is okay. Following the recipe while recreating your favorite dish is what we are here for.

It is not hard to acquire those top-secret restaurant-quality recipes. Others may advise that you need to have culinary credentials to cook those secret recipes. Yet, we can gather those ingredients ourselves and cook an elaborate meal that tastes like the real deal.

But do top secret restaurant recipes taste the way the chef served them? Perhaps. You can easily cook your favorite recipes with a little practice and patience. You would want to cook the basic formula and start adding what you think would make the recipe's flavor better after a while. You may start to think that some recipes need additional seasonings to improve your dish than the original. Nevertheless, if you wanted to prepare this dish on your own, there is still a chance.

With just a few simple tricks and tips, you can also cook quality cuisine in your kitchen. These tricks may not seem so strong on their own but can transform how you prepare and produce food when they are all used together. These tips help you cook at home like a pro from expired spices and how you use salt to arrange it before you start cooking.

When preparing desserts at home, you can tweak the recipes as you wish. As you sample the recipes, you will know the usual ingredients and techniques in making popular sweet treats. It could inspire you to create your very own recipes. You can substitute ingredients as your taste, health, or pocket dictates. You can come up, perhaps, not with a dessert that is the perfect clone of a restaurant's recipe, but with one that is exactly the way you want it to be. Most of all, the recipes here are meant for you to experience the fulfillment of seeing the smiles on the people with whom you share your creations. Keep trying and having fun with the recipes, and you will soon be reaping your sweet rewards!

If prepared food arrives outside the home, you typically have limited knowledge about salt, sugar, and processed oils. For a fact, we also apply more to our meal when it is served to the table. You will say how much salt, sugar, and oil are being used to prepare meals at home.

Copycat recipes practically give you the ability to make great restaurant food tasting in your own home and get it the right first time and easily.

CPSIA information can be obtained
at www.ICGtesting.com
Printed in the USA
LVHW051241140121
676458LV00019B/674